EXILES
AND
KINGS

EXILES
AND
KINGS

THE AFRICAN IMPRINT
ON ENGLISH CRICKET

RICHARD JONES

Dedicated to the memory of M.A.C. – a fellow cricket fan.

First published 2008

STADIA is an imprint of
The History Press Ltd
Cirencester Road, Chalford
Stroud, Gloucestershire, GL6 8PE
www.thehistorypress.co.uk

British Library Cataloguing in Publication Data.
A catalogue record for this book is available from the British Library.

ISBN 978 0 7524 4618 9
Typesetting and origination by The History Press Ltd
Printed and bound in Great Britain

CONTENTS

PHOTOGRAPHIC ACKNOWLEDGEMENTS

The majority of illustrations in this book (plates 2-6, 8-11, 14-17 and 19-23) were supplied by Patrick Eagar. For the remainder, thanks to Andrew Hignell, Les Hatton, Jim Ledbetter and the family of the late John Wallace.

INTRODUCTION

Forty summers ago, as another chapter in the Ashes story reached its conclusion, a man four years older than he was prepared to admit walked steadily to the middle of the Kennington Oval and played an innings that would change the course of English cricket history and send tremors through the core of international sporting and racial politics.

1968 saw mankind at its most brilliant and obtuse; summoning the wit and intelligence to stand ready to land upon the moon, yet lacking the insight to cope with the notion of two men with different coloured skin standing together on the same sports field. A deeply significant year in the history of the US civil rights movement – that saw the assassinations of Martin Luther King and Robert Kennedy – would end with Tommie Smith and John Carlos standing atop the Olympic medal rostrum in Mexico City, heads bowed, their black-gloved fists raised, as the strains of *The Star Spangled*

Banner drifted into the night across a stunned Estadio Olímpico Universitario. By contrast to the US where, at least in the eyes of the Supreme Court, segregationist policies were unlawful, in South Africa during 1968 the lines that could not be crossed were still clearly drawn. In England, meanwhile, Conservative MP Enoch Powell was plundering the classics in search of weaponry to deploy against the Race Relations Bill. From his vantage point in Birmingham's Midland Hotel, he could see, not the Rotunda rising from Bull Ring but the River Tiber foaming with blood. Into this quagmire stepped Basil D'Oliveira, one of the finest South African cricketers of his generation, a non-white player whose talents were banished to the rough scrubland pitches and commons of the Cape. Having lost much of his sporting prime in the search for an escape, once he had finally reached the more level playing fields of England he refused to go quietly. When D'Oliveira walked out to play his final innings in the Ashes summer of 1968, he carried onto the pitch more than just a bat. England's next scheduled engagement was a winter tour to South Africa and the political ramifications of including a man of colour in the party would be grave. Over the course of that summer, half-whispered threats and promises had buzzed around D'Oliveira, urging a strategic withdrawal from the England team. At The Oval he swatted them away with style, courage and skill – rarely has a century been scored under greater pressure.

When it was finally confirmed, D'Oliveira's selection for the tour of his homeland set in motion a sequence of events that would ultimately lead to South Africa's exile from international sport for over twenty years. Ironically, this enforced separation would draw the cricketing nations of England and South Africa together into a close relationship. A generation of world-class players, lost to Test cricket, found their place in the English counties; as the years in exile became decades some chose to pursue their international ambitions in the colours of their adopted country. At the same time, English players were heading in the opposite direction, risking censure and exile, as members of rebel touring parties.

This book looks at the modern history of English cricket through the lens of this complex and, at times, uneasy relationship, examining the impact made by a number of players from the African cricketing nations. From the traumas of the late summer of 1968, through the years of exile and rebellion, until the redemption delivered by another South African batsman at The Oval in 2005, the African imprint on English cricket is clear and indelible.

ONE

THE BEGINNING
OF THE END

At the risk of stating the obvious, cricket is a numbers game. Teams amass totals, strive for leads and chase down deficits; individual players are judged on aggregates, averages and strike-rates. Don't get me wrong, I am not suggesting that this beautifully complex sporting pursuit amounts to little more than a bean count, far from it, just that underpinning its unpredictable dramas is the unanswerable, unavoidable logic of mathematics. There are of course exceptions: certain numbers are elevated beyond the mere function of value and given status, significance, even special gifts. Take 111, for example. To English players its resemblance to a set of stumps imbues 'Nelson' with mystical, wicket-taking powers. For Australians the Jonah guaranteed to sink an innings is 87, being 13 unlucky runs short of the magic century. Let us now apply some equally strained reasoning to invest a new member of cricket's numerical hall of fame. If the calculations of Deep Thought, the omnipotent yet deeply flawed computer from *The Hitchhikers' Guide to the Galaxy*, are to be trusted, the number forty-two represents the meaning of life, the universe and everything. Subtract that number from a double century and you have the defining figure in the history of Anglo-African cricketing relations: 158 – it is where this story begins and ends.

The same could be said for The Oval, in Kennington, southeast London. It was here in August 1968 that the England Test side completed a nail-biting victory over Australia to level a difficult series. Although this result was not hugely significant in the context of the Ashes – the Australians retained the urn to continue a long winning streak – an individual performance during that match would direct the future course of cricket and sporting history. Recalled to the team after the opener R.M. Prideaux had dropped out with bronchitis, Worcestershire all-rounder Basil D'Oliveira proved the match-winner: his 158 in the first innings put England in control, and his timely intervention to remove Barry Jarman in the final hours of the contest turned the match. It was, therefore, a surprise when he was omitted from the party selected for the winter tour of South Africa, signalling the start of what Michael Melford's essay in the subsequent edition of *Wisden* referred to as the 'unpleasantness which must have been a nightmare to the ordinary sensitive lover of cricket.' Despite the official reasons for the decision – poor form during the previous winter tour of the West Indies, insufficient impact with the ball – the popular conspiracy theory centred around the political implications of selecting a 'Cape-coloured' player to tour the country of his birth, contrary to the segregationist system in South Africa at the time.

Subsequent reports of the shenanigans between John Vorster's government and the MCC (Peter Oborne's *Basil D'Oliveira. Cricket and Conspiracy: the Untold Story* highlights many unsavoury details) suggest that such theories were well-founded. In any event, the carefully constructed house of cards would soon collapse. When medium-pace bowler Tom Cartwright pulled out of the tour and D'Oliveira was drafted in as replacement, Vorster chose to interpret the move as the exercise of political rather than sporting judgement on the part of the MCC. In a speech in Bloemfontein, the prime minister rejected an attempt by certain parties 'to use sportsmen as pawns in their game to create incidents to undermine the country's way of life', and made clear that a team 'with certain political aims' would not be welcome. At which point D'Oliveira could have taken the easy option and declared himself unavailable for the tour, but he had come too far to turn back. It's a long way from the rugged pitches of the Green Point Common to the soft, spongy turf that greets a Test player as he passes through the pavilion gate at Lord's, and Basil D'Oliveira had walked every step.

Several years earlier, D'Oliveira's persistence and charm through prolonged correspondence with the great cricket journalist and broadcaster John Arlott had earned him a position as club professional with Middleton in the Lancashire League. During his first summer there he worked hard to master the alien surroundings and playing conditions (his cricket back home had invariably been played on matting), to lead Gary Sobers at the head of the season's batting averages. England clearly agreed with him – over the next four years he would age only one – and soon Worcestershire had agreed to give the 'twenty-nine-year-old' all-rounder a chance in first-class cricket.

D'Oliveira immediately set about the task of repaying their faith. In his first Championship match against Essex, faced with indigenous English conditions and bowlers that knew how to exploit them, he played the kind of innings that would become his hallmark. On a mission to serve the team, rather than a quest in search of personal glories, D'Oliveira allied supreme natural talents with patience borne out of a desperation to succeed and progress. His autobiography explains the basic philosophy as follows: 'As a boy I aimed to hit every ball into the road. Now I give the first hour of every innings to the bowler. He can do what he likes with it, as long as he doesn't get me out... The first hour is his. I am cautious, but not worried. The second hour is mine. That is when I begin to take over.'

Although Worcestershire could only draw the game, the contribution of their new all-rounder – 153 runs, thirty tidy overs yielding three wickets – was loaded with promise. And they would soon call on it; a slow start to the season argued against a successful defence of their County Championship title but, thanks in no small part to the prolific middle-order partnership developed between D'Oliveira and Tom Graveney, Worcestershire would finish the season marginally ahead of the pack. Even though D'Oliveira would have celebrated the team success far above his personal achievements, his 1,500 Championship runs at an average of 43, 35 wickets and an equal number of catches must have provided immense satisfaction. As would the knowledge that the only names above his in that year's list of Championship batting averages belonged to seasoned Test players: Cowdrey, Graveney, Parfitt and Edrich. Soon enough he would be joining them.

England had two unlikely sporting heroes in the summer of 1966. At Wembley, Tofik Bakhramov played a blinder out wide on the right to set up the home side's crucial third goal in a football match against West Germany, while on the cricket field Basil D'Oliveira (at times almost single-handedly) took the fight to the formidable West Indians. Named as twelfth man for the first Test, D'Oliveira was doubly blessed, avoiding as he did the shocking reversal suffered by his colleagues at Old Trafford meant that he would make his Test debut at Lord's. Here England would regain some pride, forcing the tourists to battle for a draw. The contribution of their debutant – timely and understated – adding significant value to the team effort. With the ball he was first miserly, then incisive, removing Seymour Nurse to curtail the West Indian first innings. With the bat he simply stuck to his method, drawing the venom from an attack led by a rampant Wes Hall before looking to impose himself. In the context of the match his twenty-seven runs were vital but perhaps more significantly, he proved he had the heart and stomach for a fight. He would call on these reserves frequently that summer, all too often the last man standing on a burning deck, D'Oliveira's battling half centuries in the matches at Trent Bridge and Headingley postponed rather than prevented defeats. Naming him one of their cricketers of the year, *Wisden* recognised that: 'England had gained not only a skilful cricketer but a man of rare fighting qualities… As he grows in confidence and experience in the Test sphere England could find themselves with one of the finest all-rounders in post-war cricket.'

The following summer he set out to fulfil this prophecy, starting with a debut Test century against the Indians at Leeds. Once again, the team ethic dictated his approach, crashing a swift century to accelerate England into a dominant position. D'Oliveira's effort earned him the Walter Lawrence Trophy for the fastest century of the year. By contrast, Boycott's epic 246 brought him the sack. A brace of important fifties during the second series of the summer against Pakistan saw

D'Oliveira finish the season with a Test average in the mid-sixties and a berth for the trip to the Caribbean that winter.

His form during the tour slipped far below his usual high standard, an honest appraisal of the cause is recorded in Peter Oborne's book: 'The hospitality was out of this world, everyone was nice to me, I was gullible and just accepted it all. I had too much to drink, I lived too well, I did everything that was wrong… I cocked the whole thing up.' These days, such indiscretions would probably have shrieked from the back pages of the tabloids but at the time nothing was said publicly. However, the insinuation that D'Oliveira was an 'unreliable tourist' would later resurface, as the MCC sought to justify their decision to overlook him for their tour to South Africa the following winter.

To the casual observer, D'Oliveira's 1968 season appeared to reject the established laws of sport in favour of a more random, existentialist approach – success was punished, failure rewarded. The collective failure of the English batsmen at Old Trafford handed the first Test to Australia but D'Oliveira was the least culpable, battling away for nearly three hours on the final day trying to save the game, he eventually ran out of partners 13 short of a century. Unlucky for some, despite being the only batsman that had shown the form and fight that England would need if they harboured genuine ambitions of regaining the Ashes, he was dropped. Denied the challenge of top-flight competition and beset by whispered threats and promises regarding his intentions for the forthcoming winter tour of his homeland, his form deserted him. In the weeks that followed he would fail to reach double figures on no fewer than thirteen occasions; his number appeared to be up. But he need not have worried, his script for that summer was written by Shakespeare – 'There's a divinity that shapes our ends, rough-hew them how we will' – not *Wisden*. Sure enough, following a remarkable series of last-minute withdrawals on the eve of the final Test, England came calling.

The match produced an exciting finish but would not, under different circumstances, have left an indelible print on the history of English cricket. The destiny of the Ashes was not an issue and a sizeable century from John Edrich had put the home side in control of the match from day one. But it was the century scored on day two, Friday 23 August 1968, which would change everything. As ever, D'Oliveira began watchfully, assessing the conditions, appraising the attack; later he would wield the bat more freely, fighting his way out of a corner in pursuit of 158 brilliant, cathartic, historic runs. As the scoreboard ticked away merrily, a political time-bomb rolled into place between the MCC and the South African Cricket Association; out in the middle, the ball raced across the grass and the pigeons scattered.

Although the century at The Oval undoubtedly represented the defining moment of D'Oliveira's sporting life, it was by no means the final significant point in his career as a Test cricketer. During the matches that followed he would, as before, fulfil a role beyond value in any English sporting team: the 'good man in a crisis.' An unbeaten century in Dacca, during the 1968/69 tour of Pakistan, saved England in a series best described as difficult; the phlegmatic summary of the third Test in Karachi provided on the excellent Cricket Archive website – 'The match was abandoned due to riots shortly before lunch on day three' – says it all. This ability to perform under trying conditions would ensure that D'Oliveira's place in England's Ashes history would not be limited to the century that squared the 1968 series.

The portents for English success in the return match in 1970/71 were not good. They had not won an Ashes series since Laker's summer of 1956 and no side had recovered the urn on Australian soil since Douglas Jardine had employed some infamously robust tactics during the 1932/33 encounter. With the first two matches drawn and the third washed-out, England seized the initiative at Sydney. A crucial century partnership between Boycott and D'Oliveira in the second innings opened the door; John Snow kicked it down, ripping through the Australian order to finish with figures of 7-40. With the Ashes apparently in their grasp, England were suddenly clutching at thin air in Melbourne at 88/3, over 400 runs adrift. Again D'Oliveira steadied the ship, composing a century in just under six hours and forming partnerships first with Luckhurst, then the skipper Illingworth, to guide England to safety. Thirty-four years later, a century from a South African-born batsman in the fifth Test of a tight Ashes series would, once again, represent a key moment in returning the urn to England after a prolonged absence.

A playing career in English cricket that began with Middleton in 1960 finally came to an end in May 1980 as D'Oliveira took a last bow for Worcestershire in their County Championship match with Middlesex. Although his birthday had always been a moveable feast-day, the half century was clearly within sight by the time he eventually called time. His contribution to his adopted county was immense. Always a reliable performer with bat and ball, in 1974 – the year his old sparring partner from the Lancashire League, Gary Sobers, retired – D'Oliveira's runs and wickets helped the county to snatch the Championship from Hampshire. As coach, he would oversee two further titles in 1988 and 1989. Worcestershire have won the Championship five times in their history, four of those victories owed much to his skill and enthusiasm. But to analyse the impact made by D'Oliveira on English cricket in statistical terms is too simplistic, too formulaic, we have to set the numbers to one side. Put simply it is the notion of sport as a unifying force that owes the greatest debt to the man who honed his cricketing skills on the testing, uneven playing fields of the Cape.

TWO

PUBLIC ENEMY NO.1

In the summer of 1970, as the world of football exploded into brilliant colour across television screens around the globe – the iconic, golden team of Pelé and Jairzinho beguiling the Azures across the verdant turf of the Azteca Stadium – cricket's obsession with black and white cast a long shadow across the game. The fall-out from the D'Oliveira affair two years earlier had left relations between the cricket authorities in England and South Africa delicately poised, 1970 would be the tipping point. With public opinion stiffening against the segregationist policies prevailing in South Africa, the 'Stop the Seventy Tour' campaign led by Peter Hain (the future MP and government minister, then a young man whose family had come to England to escape the Apartheid regime) gathered pace. Under increasing pressure the MCC cancelled their engagement with the Springboks scheduled for that summer. The hastily arranged replacement series between England and a Rest of the World XI provided a feast for cricket fans, together with a cold side-order of irony for the politicians to chew over. The Rest of the World side saw four white South Africans join stars from Pakistan and India under the captaincy of a West Indian; in D'Oliveira, the England team already included a 'Cape-coloured' in their ranks, they now added 6ft 7in of blonde South African in the form of Tony Greig.

Although the Sussex all-rounder would, like D'Oliveira, later find himself caught in the eye of a storm that sent tremors through the foundations of the English cricketing establishment, the similarities between the two men ended there. While the unassuming D'Oliveira was essentially a victim of circumstance, Greig's tribulations were often of his own design. He enraged fast bowlers into acts of murderous retribution, engendered resentment in his native and adopted countries by electing to play Test cricket for the latter, and was ultimately vilified as a charlatan and a mercenary for his part in the establishment of Kerry Packer's World Series Cricket. He was, of course, an all-rounder. Charismatic and eloquent, his penchant for straight talking charmed and excited the media, while a dogged competitive streak earned him the respect of teammates and opponents alike. As England captain, he exemplified the qualities that a successful side must ally to the talent at its disposal, scattering a handful of Southern Hemispheric grit over the laudable, but too often fallible, English sporting mores of playing the game.

Although Greig began the series against the Rest of the World well – he collected the scalps of Sobers and Barry Richards in each innings of the first match – subsequent performances with bat and ball were less convincing and he was omitted from the touring party bound for Australia that winter. Ironically, this new round in the battle for the Ashes degenerated into a war of attrition that would have ideally suited Greig's style and approach. As it was, Ray Illingworth's men prevailed thanks in no small part to the belligerent, incessant and often brilliant batting of Geoffrey Boycott. Although the selectors stuck with the winning side throughout the following summer, Greig would find a route back into the England team by treading the same path that had originally taken him there – a Rest of the World tour. As a member of the side that toured Australia under the leadership of Sobers in the winter of 1971/72, Greig was able to advance his case on two counts. Firstly, he proved himself consistently with bat and ball against the players that would provide England's opposition the following summer. Secondly, he held down the all-rounder's spot in the World side ahead of Yorkshire's Richard Hutton – son of the great Leonard and the man he needed to supplant to regain a place in the England team. With Hutton staggering under the burden of expectation he inevitably carried throughout his career and D'Oliveira gradually regaining the years he had 'lost' after arriving in English cricket, the selectors recognised that backing the twenty-five-year-old Greig offered the greatest value. A much-maligned breed, the selectors' judgement proved sound in both the long and short term; Greig collected five wickets and a brace of half centuries in the match, and a further fifty-seven consecutive Test caps during the following five years that saw him glide into the centre of English sporting life. The dramatic events that ultimately ended this run were, of course, beyond the imagination of everyone.

Equally unimaginable to followers of English cricket during the past twenty years is the fanciful notion of their side stringing together back-to-back Ashes victories – the solitary success during this period merely representing a momentary respite from a sustained and very painful beating. By contrast, during the 1970s and 1980s, the old argument was far less one-sided, with the urn changing hands regularly. In the 1970/71 encounter, Ray Illingworth's side began a new chapter by wresting the honour back from Australia on their home turf and retaining it with a draw in the return series in England during 1972. However, rather like Mike Gatting (the next and, at the time of writing, last England captain to succeed Down Under), Illingworth's tenure as skipper ended abruptly, leaving the Ashes door ajar. By the mid-1970s it was hanging off its hinges, hammered mercilessly by an Antipodean bowling attack that coupled skill with venomous pace. At the same time the West Indies were developing a lethal arsenal of their own that would terrorise batsmen around the world for more than a decade. To survive and prosper in this dangerous new world – the editorial for the 1975 edition of *Wisden* warned of the 'Menace of Short Pitched Bouncers' – England required a captain with the stomach for a fight, who relished the challenge of playing the game on the edge. An incident during the winter tour of 1972/73 suggested that in Tony Greig they had found such a man. Although England lost the rubber in disappointing fashion after winning the first Test in Delhi, the tour was a marked personal success for the young all-rounder: a maiden Test century at Bombay contributed to an average of over sixty and some useful wickets earned him the award as man of the series. The flashpoint that revealed the keenness of the competitive edge to his game came in the third Test in Madras, when the Indian skipper Ajit Wadekar edged the ball into Greig's hands at slip. With no reaction from the umpire or batsman the fielder decided to take matters into his own hands, as he recalls in his autobiography: 'Several of our lads showed a degree of anger, but for me it was just too much. I raced down the pitch, brandishing the ball above my head and shrieking at the umpire.' Wadekar was given out. The outburst would earn Greig an appointment at Lord's on his return but his reputation as a leader was established – the captaincy of Sussex followed and for England's next winter tour the man from the Cape was installed as vice-captain of his adopted country.

Even before the touring party had reached the Caribbean the storm clouds had started to gather. The English summer had ended in controversy over the demotion of Illingworth following a home series defeat to the West Indies. The widely held assumption that the reins would then be handed to Geoffrey Boycott was confounded by the appointment of Mike Denness as skipper, with Greig as his deputy. The ramifications of this decision were to direct the cricketing careers of all three men in significantly different directions. The surprise elevation of Denness – a useful county bats-man many felt ill-equipped for the rigours of Test captaincy – ultimately proved his downfall. Successive batterings at the hands of Australia slowly, painfully cost him the faith of his players, the confidence of the public and the support of the selectors. Boycott's response was less predictable, withdraw-ing his services after the first Test of the summer of 1974, he entered a period of self-imposed exile that would last for over three years. For Greig, the tour presented a series of challenges and competing priorities that would test his mettle both on and off the field. With the camp divided over the captaincy issue, the task of uniting the players behind the skipper fell to his lieutenant; then, of course, there was the incidental matter of taking on the West Indies on their home turf. As ever, in adversity he thrived, keeping Boycott on-side to guide the top order, scoring valuable runs himself and using initiative and skill to produce a healthy crop of wickets on the unforgiving, sun-baked pitches on the Caribbean islands. His success on both fronts was exemplified in the fifth Test at Trinidad where he added thirteen wickets to the century and 99 scored by Boycott to secure a famous victory and level the series. In the tour scorebook Greig's haul of twenty-four wickets looks impressive; in reality it was near miraculous. Frustrated at the impotence of his medium pacers early in the rubber, he reinvented himself as an off-spinner during the third Test in Barbados, taking six wickets to add to his score of 148, and never looked back. Perhaps more than any other figure in the history of English sport, Greig understood the maxim described by H.G. Wells as 'nature's inexorable imperative' – adapt or perish.

Sadly no amount of spin could disguise the bitter facts of the reversal England were to suffer in their next serious engagement – the 1974/75 Ashes tour. In a series dominated by pace, the Australians had the ultimate partnership, Lillee and Thomson – phonetically a sweet little old lady, in reality two angry young men hell-bent on bombing the English batsman back to the Stone Age. Why? Well aside from the usual tensions underpinning any Ashes series, the flames of this particular bout were fanned at the earliest opportunity by Greig. Frustrated at the courtesy shown by the English fast bowlers to the Australian lower order during the first Test, he slammed in a short delivery to Lillee that spat off the pitch and threatened to bury itself in his moustache. The ball caught a glove raised in self-defence and flew into the welcoming embrace of Knott behind the stumps. Greig knew that he had breached an unwritten code – fast bowlers' union and all that – and Lillee's comments to him as he passed en route to the pavilion left little to the imagination. The game was on.

England' response was unconvincing and a first-innings collapse seemed inevitable as Greig strode to the crease as public enemy no.1. Having withstood the initial barrage with care, he started to bat more freely, revelling in the role of pantomime villain, he played up to the crowd, signalling his own boundaries with a disdainful wave of hand. The fans bayed, the bowling got progressively shorter but Greig kept his nerve and head, brazening it out for a dogged century. It proved to be one of the few highlights of a tour that saw England's batsman out ABH almost as often as lbw. With only a token victory in the final Test to his name, the pressure on Mike Denness grew. Ill health and poor form cast him as a somewhat peripheral figure on tour – haunted by the back-to-back Ashes successes of the Illingworth era glowing brightly in a lost, golden past. To make matters worse, the Australians repainted their Indian sign over Denness's men the following summer, bowling England out for double figures in the semi-final of the inaugural World Cup, before extending their stay for four further Tests matches.

So many sports played at the highest level are often won and lost on the finest of margins, the backhand passing shot that kisses the line, the perfect penalty that grazes the inside of the post, the pitch that catches the cup, not the bunker. Cricket adds further complexity in the shape of extraneous, yet vital factors that even the most sublimely talented player cannot influence be it the state of the pitch, the mood of the weather, the toss of a coin. All three conspired against England during the summer of 1975, starting at Edgbaston where Mike Denness called correctly at the toss and following careful consultation, offered the tourists first use of the pitch. In more recent times Denness's successors have suffered the same sinking feeling that followed during the first day of an Ashes series. On day one of the 2002/03 tussle, Nasser Hussain watched Hayden and Ponting rattle up 364 at Brisbane; four years later on the same ground it was 346 from Ponting and Hussey that ruined a day for Andrew Flintoff that had started badly enough when his premier fast bowler's first ball had sought him out at second slip.

Back in 1975, vilified by the media for his judgement, Denness's fate was sealed by the elements. Having watched Australia reach 359, the home skipper then saw his openers chased back to the pavilion by rain only minutes into their reply. These days the 'Brumbrella' would be deployed to protect and preserve the Edgbaston wicket; in a less scientific era the batsmen took their chances and the bowlers cleaned up. Lillee and Thomson took five apiece in each innings as England lost without requiring their opponents to bat again. Appointed for only the first match of the series, in many eyes Denness was already a dead man walking. For round two at Lord's, the home of cricket and bastion of Englishness, the side would be led by a South African.

Never a man to suffer self-doubt, the resulting wave of optimism that swept around the country in the wake of his appointment did at least provide Greig with some cause for concern, as he recalls in his autobiography:

We were in an abysmal run and the public wanted to see something new, something different. Maybe I had the personality and the physical appearance which fitted their wish, but it got to the point when I wanted to turn on the well-wishers and ask them what they expected me to do.

In typical Greig style, his next move was entirely unexpected. With the Australian pace attack at their marks, pawing the turf, hungry for blood, it was at the captain's instigation a man who, on the face of it, looked like the ultimate victim was drafted into the England top order. David Steele, a thirty-three-year-old journeyman from the county circuit, with prematurely grey hair and wire-rimmed glasses, looked more like a world-class librarian than batsman. If this was England's secret weapon in disguise, my God it was a good disguise.

The greeting he received from Thomson, when arriving for the first time at the crease, pithily encapsulated the Australian disbelief: 'Who's this, then? Father-fucking-Christmas?'

The answer to the first question was relayed over the remaining matches of the summer. A desperately awkward-looking specimen, given no prayer of success, Steele was every inch the quintessential English sporting hero. Hunched at the crease, peering through beer-bottle lenses at the angry red orb hurtling towards him, his defiant, courageous and highly skilful performances during the series helped to return a measure of pride to English cricket and would earn him the title of BBC Sports Personality of the Year. Thomson's incredulity at the sight that greeted him on that first morning of the Lord's Test was no doubt sharpened by the suspense created by Steele's delayed arrival in the middle.

Whether it was the tension of a belated international debut, unfamiliarity with the labyrinthine interior of the Lord's pavilion or simply bat-eyed vision, Steele famously took a wrong turn en route to the fray, descended an extra flight of steps and found himself in the bowels of HQ staring at a row of Victorian dunnies. Strewth. Like Scott and Thesiger before him, a mere wrong turning was not enough to dampen the spirits of a true English hero; when he finally made it to the middle, with hoots of Antipodean derision ringing in his ears, Steele settled to the task of hauling his country out of the pit. Joined by Greig with the score on 49/4, the pair put on 96 priceless runs, and when John Snow tore through the tourist's batting line-up the following morning England were suddenly, quite unexpectedly, back in the hunt.

Although the Australians would hang on to draw the Test, England's newfound purpose and confidence – not to mention their greying, bespectacled flashing blade – would again take the fight to the tourists in the third match at Headingley. With sizeable contributions from Steele in each innings and Snow's pace complementing the left-arm spin of debutant Phil Edmonds, the home side looked like warm favourites at the close of play on day four. Now the vagaries of cricket entered unchartered territory. Having seen his predecessor sunk by the coin in the first Test, Greig was blessed by the weather on the final morning of the third – gunmetal skies over Leeds suggested a bowler's day – but damned by the pitch, in the most unpredictable and dramatic fashion.

During the night, as part of the ongoing campaign to release George Davis – an East End cab driver jailed for armed robbery on evidence subsequently considered to be unreliable – vandals had broken into the ground, dug up sections of the wicket and doused it with oil. With no further play possible, England had lost their last chance of regaining the Ashes. The oil poured onto the Headingley turf effectively ended a turbulent summer for English cricket. With no tour scheduled to fill the winter months, Greig and his side could relax and recuperate ahead of their meeting the following summer with the West Indies. A meeting that would, thanks to an inflammatory comment by their skipper, test their resolve and reflexes to the full.

Bragging in public ahead of important sporting fixtures is a dangerous game – just ask the former England football manager Graham Taylor. On the eve of the 1992 European Football Championships, his grinning face filled the front page of a tabloid newspaper assuring the nation that victory was a trifling formality. A fortnight later, after England had been bombed out by Sweden having mustered only one goal in the entire tournament, a juxtaposition of Taylor's head and a turnip appeared on the back of the same newspaper above the headline 'Swedes 2 – Turnip 1'.

Despite a relatively successful career as a club manager with Watford and Aston Villa, being likened to a root vegetable (and appearing in a television documentary capturing the full glory of his expletive-laden desperation at international level) is most likely to endure as Taylor's legacy to the beautiful game for many observers. Equally, while Tony Greig may be remembered as a gifted and courageous batsman, more-than-useful bowler and an inspirational leader, his televised promise to make the West Indies 'grovel' is an indelible stain on his CV. In view of the political climate prevailing at the time, Greig's South African provenance only served to fan the inferno. In his autobiography Viv Richards observes wryly how, as soon as word reached the Caribbean of Greig's vow, motivational team talks became an irrelevance. That summer the gentleman's game would live up to the Orwellian ideal, war minus the shooting.

Even so, the tourists had to wait until the third Test was played out on a bumpy deck at Old Trafford to serve up their chilled, Jamaica Dutch pot of revenge. For starters, Roberts, Holding and Daniel tore through the English order in 32.5 ferocious overs at the paltry cost of 71 runs. Centuries from Greenidge and Richards in the second innings left England a tantalising target of 552 runs to chase to secure victory. Now the fun began in earnest. Batting to save the game, and by all accounts their lives, the elderly opening pair of Close (aged forty-five) and Edrich (thirty-nine) were peppered with a barrage of bouncers for the final excruciating hour-and-a-half of play on Saturday. On seeing Close's torso exposed in the dressing room that evening, spinner Pat Pocock remarked: 'It was as if someone had forced handfuls of marbles under his skin.' The West Indies duly won the match, the following two Tests and thus a 3-0 series victory.

Although Greig strenuously refuted the supposition that his comments had carried any racial connotations – his autobiography explains: 'All I had intended to convey during the interview was that there were two teams due to play in the Tests series… in my enthusiasm to drum up some support for England, I simply used an unfortunate word' – he was clearly a sportsman who understood the psychological aspects of game play. Carefully chosen and timely words to teammates and opponents alike characterised his approach to competition, just as much as his ethos of leading by example in times of adversity. Both qualities were evident during the winter tour to India that followed the drubbing at the hands of the West Indies.

For reasons unknown to anyone at the time, Greig included, that series would be his last as captain of England. As a rising star in the colours of his adopted country, his performances during the previous tour of the subcontinent had cemented his place in the side and established a reputation as future captain material. His abiding memory of the trip was, however, a negative one; the bitter disappointment of seeing a 1-0 series lead slip away as the Indians rallied and ultimately beat the tourists still rankled with him, and he was steely in his determination that a side under his stewardship would not suffer a similar fate. When history repeated itself and the visitors took first blood at Delhi, Greig chose a team gathering on Christmas night to take matters into his own hands. His tour diary recalls: 'Something was necessary to jolt them back into an awareness of priorities, and I elected for a verbal assault. When I am angry, my language can deteriorate. That night it was appalling…' The shock tactics appeared to work. In the second match in Calcutta, batting first by choice, the Indians were all out for 155. By the end of day two, however, England seemed destined for a similar fate at 90/4, writhing in a web of deceit spun by the mercurial Bishen Bedi, with Tolchard and the captain unbeaten overnight. Unbeaten, at least by the bowlers, shortly after midnight Greig awoke bathed in sweat, running a high fever. In spite of the medication provided at 3 a.m. by the team medic Bernie Thomas, the captain was already a centurion of sorts by the time he wobbled back onto the field at the start of the following day's play, carrying with him a temperature of 104. That he was still there when the stumps were drawn, having spent the entire day in the broiling cauldron of Calcutta's Eden Gardens stadium, battling the demons of spin and with his innards in uproar speaks volumes about the qualities that Greig, at his best, brought to the role of England cricket captain. The rest day brought peace – a press conference from his bed was the main event – but when battle was rejoined the following day his century and a white-hot spell from Bob Willis pushed the away side to the brink of victory. The crowd turned ugly, the Indians capitulated and, for the first time since Douglas Jardine's tour of 1933/34, England were crowned kings of the subcontinent.

Of course, crowns, like halos, have a tendency to slip. Lauded for his performances and leadership skills in India and further celebrated for a spirited and promising performance in the Centenary Test during the homeward stopover in Melbourne, Greig's stock had never been higher. His fall from grace and subsequent casting as a sporting and social pariah was sudden. Although the Centenary Test had provided a tasty aperitif for the main Ashes battle that was to follow during the English summer, the event had also seen a frenzy of activity behind the scenes as the biggest revolution in cricket history started to take shape. Australian media magnate Kerry Packer was busy assembling the cast of high-profile players destined to perform in his World Series Cricket 'circus' and, when Greig met up with him in Melbourne, ostensibly to discuss possible future broadcasting work on Packer's Channel 9 Network, the captaincy of the World side was offered. Greig's acceptance and later involvement in the process of sounding out other English Test players placed him squarely at the centre of the controversy when the story finally broke. Quite apart from the threat to the established order posed by the plan, the covert nature of the operation fuelled the inferno of outrage, disgust and self-righteousness that raged within the cricketing establishment and, of course, the media.

Clearly not a decision he took lightly, Greig justified his chosen path primarily by reference to a desire to improve the lot of the professional cricketer, seeing his own relatively uncertain future (even as captain of the national team) as the perfect example. The financial incentives and future employment opportunities that Packer could offer to Greig far exceeded the returns that the remainder of his conventional professional cricket career could deliver. For the game as a whole, he saw World Series Cricket as a necessary wake-up call – a chance to exploit commercial possibilities and take cricket to a new level for players and spectators alike. To a certain extent his view was supported by news of a sponsorship deal between the TCCB and Cornhill Insurance, announced within months of the Packer story breaking, that would provide a significant revenue boost to the English game and players. Whatever he may have gained, Greig's decision left a palpable sense of personal loss: 'My biggest wrench was the sacrifice of the England captaincy when I was on the threshold of my great remaining ambition in the game – to lead an Ashes-winning side.'

As it was, he would retain his place in a side led by Mike Brearley – another captain well versed in the art of sports psychology – that went on to reclaim the urn during an epochal summer for English cricket that also saw Boycott return to score his hundredth first-class century at Headingley and Botham's first Test. Even then, for Greig the murmurings at his retention in the team and a direct involvement in the High Court restraint of trade action brought by the World Series Cricket consortium against the cricketing authorities soured the sweet taste of success.

For many, this final episode in a colourful and often controversial playing career overshadows the contribution made by Tony Greig to English cricket. This is perhaps unfair. As the first man to score 3,000 runs and take 100 wickets in official Tests for England, his record as an all-rounder stands the test of time; only Botham and Flintoff have followed him so far. Although his record as captain appears relatively modest, at least in statistical terms (won three, lost five, drew six) his role in turning a struggling group of players – divided by the captaincy issue and bereft of their best batsman – into a team able to triumph on the subcontinent and regain the Ashes cannot be overlooked.

THREE

THE REAL THING

It is the summer of 1963 and a small crowd has gathered spontaneously on the pavement outside the Sportsman's Club in Tottenham Court Road. At its centre the Olympic Light Heavyweight Champion is explaining in precise yet lyrical terms the extent of the damage he proposes to inflict on the local favourite. Two schoolboys step forward to make a nervous request for an autograph. The smiling giant accepts pen and paper from the first and, unable to place the boy's accent, asks where he is from. The response prompts a sudden change in the big man's demeanour; the smile fades, the paper is signed and swiftly returned, he turns away. The boxer – then known as Cassius Clay, later Muhammad Ali – became the greatest sporting icon of the twentieth century. The second boy, denied an autograph, was Barry Richards, the most naturally gifted batsman that South Africa has ever produced. The mood of this chance meeting exemplifies the problems that would subsequently blight their careers, as the politics of race and sport conspired to deny both Ali and Richards the best years of their sporting lives.

Despite a major scare in the fourth round, Ali lived up to his sidewalk sideshow by stopping Henry Cooper in the fifth at Wembley Stadium in June 1963. The following year he delivered on his promise to 'shock the world' by relieving the supposedly insuperable Sonny Liston of the World Heavyweight crown. Nine title defences followed in four years of pugilism and poetry. Here was an athlete at the very top of his game, charming the media, battering opponents, hauling in the crowds. As the journalist Hunter S. Thompson observed cheerily: 'He came, he saw, and if he didn't entirely conquer – he came as close as anybody we are likely to see in the lifetime of this doomed generation.' When, in the spring of 1967 at the height of his powers, Ali was finally stopped, the culprit was not a meaty hook or right cross but something considerably more potent – politics. An 'evasion' of the Vietnam draft, following his conversion to Islam, saw Ali stripped of his title and cast into the boxing wilderness between March 1967 and October 1970, his peak years, many have argued. The celebrated bouts that followed his return – the Rumble in the Jungle, the brutal Frazier trilogy – owed more to endurance, heart and a canny sense of ring craft and less to the dancing feet and quick hands that characterised his early years.

On the day that Ali stepped through the ropes in Atlanta to re-enter the world of professional boxing against Jerry Quarry, Barry Richards was taking centre stage at the Adelaide Oval, guiding South Australia to a Sheffield Shield Trophy draw against Western Australia. Later that season, during the return fixture, he would reach his apotheosis with the willow, scoring 325 runs in a single day against a bowling attack sharpened by the raw fury of a youthful Dennis Lillee. As his autobiography reveals: 'Recalling that innings now is like a dream. Somehow I managed to sustain for a complete day the sort of form that usually materialises in short, glorious moments.'

In truth, in the two years leading up to that golden day in Perth, Richards had been accumulating runs with a style and rapacity that transcended mere 'form'. It began with a promise made during a television interview to score 2,000 runs in 1968, his debut season in England playing for Hampshire. In the same way that Ali's pre-fight predictions rankled with some in the boxing world, Richards's confidence in his own ability whipped up a frenzy of emotions within the normally staid ranks of county cricket; eyebrows were raised and the occasional tut heard. The generous financial package that Hampshire had offered this young, luxuriously talented import had also been noted. As Richards walked out to bat for his debut Championship innings at Hove, the level of expectation amongst the players, crowd and watching media was intense. In his defence, Richards would later explain that his stated aspiration was the product of rough arithmetic – multiplying his run-rate the previous season with Natal by the likely number of innings during a full season of county cricket – rather than the arrogance of youth. In any event his opening gambit in that first encounter with Sussex, facing the pace and guile of John Snow on a lively wicket, was inauspicious. He did trouble the scorers – someone had to perform the task of describing a circle in the 'runs' column next to his name – but not too much. As the twenty-two-year-old pretender trudged back to the pavilion the outfield hissed with muttered references to his pre-season prediction.

Life got dramatically worse, then much better. A toilet brush to the eye during high jinks that night in the team hotel was followed by an unbeaten fifty in the second innings of the match, and another against Yorkshire's Trueman and Illingworth in the following fixture on a damp, treacherous track at Harrogate. Then an experimental elevation to the top of the order during the match with Northampton at the end of May brought instant success – a century in each innings. The man later described by Sir Donald Bradman as 'the world's best-ever right-handed opener' had found his place. By the time that Hampshire arrived at Westcliff-on-Sea in mid-July, Richards had passed the halfway point in his quest for the magic total, however, the lively batting strip that saw the home side skittled out without reaching three figures suggested that little further progress would be possible at Chalkwell Park. As it was, judicious shot selection and some nimble footwork paid handsome dividends; Richards's 176 from a total of 301 proved to be a match-winning effort.

Although Hampshire's form would be indifferent over the remainder of the season, their young opener continued to impress, and his wicket soon became highly prized. One can only imagine, then, that when Carlton Forbes saw his delivery nick Richards's inside edge en route to the wickets early in the first innings of the match against Nottinghamshire at Portsmouth, he would have breathed a sigh of relief. One can also speculate at the stream of curses he aired as the ball ricocheted off the stumps without dislodging the bails. And raced to the boundary. How Forbes and his colleagues must have chuckled at the vicissitudes of fate (not to mention the solidity of the turf housing the stumps at the United Services Recreation Ground) as they watched Richards progress from 29 to a career-best 206. In doing so he passed his self-imposed target and would finish the campaign as its most prolific batsmen with only Boycott improving on his average.

Richards' spectacular debut season in England, during a summer where the wet conditions had generally favoured the ball over the bat, was duly recognised with a nomination as one of *Wisden*'s five cricketers of the year. Justifying his selection, the editor of the almanack, Norman Preston, signed off his appraisal thus: 'Richards' horizons seem limit-less, and it will be fascinating to see how far his talents will take him. Few, anywhere in the world, have his possibili-ties.' Ironically, it was the controversy alluded to in Preston's opening remarks of the same edition – 'At a time when we admire the American astronauts who encircled the moon on Christmas Day, we have to record... the petty squabbles of men on Earth.' – that would, ultimately, limit both Richards horizons and his possibilities. The day before the young open-er's dashing double century at Portsmouth, at The Oval Basil D'Oliveira had played the seminal innings of his career and, unwittingly, penned the opening lines of a deeply significant chapter in the history of cricket.

Selected for his Test debut to face an England side that would never arrive in South Africa, Richards instead applied himself to Natal's challenge for the Currie Cup. Although the province endured a moderate season, their young opener, deploying new skills acquired on the often erratic pitches of an English summer, enjoyed personal successes finishing with 565 runs at 56.50. Back in England monsoon-like conditions in May and a series of disruptive injuries meant that his return to the South Coast for a second lap of the county circuit was, initially, less rewarding. However, following a pattern that was evident throughout his career, the sight of opponents of an international calibre would awaken his talent. Presented with the West Indian tourists at Southampton he improved upon his 86 in the first innings with an unbeaten 120 in the second to set up a sporting, if ultimately unsuccessful, Hampshire declaration. After a lean time in the two Championship matches that followed, the challenge of taking on Test players again proved the necessary inspiration as he helped himself to 132 from the New Zealand tourists. Richards didn't look back. In the five remaining fixtures of the Championship season he made up for the earlier setbacks with centuries against Lancashire and Northants and half centuries in the other three games.

For the second year in succession Hampshire finished in a respectable fifth place in the Championship and only lost out to Lancashire by a single point in the inaugural Sunday League, a competition welcomed with a typically prescient comment by Norman Preston: 'The public have already shown their appreciation of the clear-cut single-day contest and one wonders whether the Championship itself and even Test matches will retain their appeal without change in some form of the maximum number of overs permitted.' On a personal level Richards had again excelled finishing the season in the upper reaches of the batting averages, thanks largely to his resurgence in the second half of the summer.

The hot streak continued into the following South African season; three centuries in the four Currie Cup games that preceded the arrival of the Australian touring party cemented his place in the side for the opening Test. Cleaning up in the county and provincial leagues was one thing, Bill Lawry's side would present challenges on an entirely different level. Of specific concern to a young opening batsman was the range of questions that the bowling attack promised to pose; even if the opening pair of McKenzie and Connolly had been negotiated safely that would only usher in the guile and variety of the spinners Mallett and Gleeson. Long before Muttiah Muralitharan's magic arm threw the ICC biomechanical department into a spin, Johnnie Gleeson's sleight of hand redefined the art of spin bowling, leading Richie Benaud to rate him alongside Bosanquet, Iverson and Warne as one of the four practitioners to have 'broken the mould and made batsmen think seriously about what was coming down the pitch at them.' In Gleeson's case the magician's wand was his middle finger, which he used to dictate the direction of the spin on the ball in the instant before release.

Even with these potent weapons at their disposal, the tourists made slow progress through the South African order in the first innings of the opening Test. By contrast the Australian response saw wickets fall at regular intervals with only Doug Walters and the two spinners providing any resistance. With over 200 runs in the bank Richards set the tone for the home side's second innings with a brisk 32 from 44 balls. Once again the depth of the batting paid off, leaving the Australians with little hope of a positive outcome. The target was 450 for a shock victory, or conversely, dig in and try to hold at bay a team returning from exile, ravenous for victory. It was undeniably no contest.

It got worse. Batting first on a true surface at Kingsmead in the second match the Springboks had amassed 622 before inviting their guests to try their luck. Although the most eye-catching entry on the card is Graeme Pollock's epic 274, the contribution by the first man in was the choice of the purist. Having scored 94 before lunch, Richards celebrated his first Test century with a flurry of attacking strokes. To the spectator it was a work of art: 'A glittering and technically perfect innings of 140, the equal of which has rarely been seen,' Geoffrey A. Chettle reported in *Wisden*; to its architect a self-admonishing refrain that: 'I should have set myself for 200, but I tried to whack every ball.' Richards had experienced a tantalising taste of sporting immortality. A debut Test century, exhilarating and elegant in equal measure, in front of his home crowd against formidable opponents; it doesn't get any better than that. And for Richards, it never would.

Although the first day of the third Test at the Wanderers presented the beleaguered Australians with a brief window of opportunity – edged chances went to hand, but then to turf – Richards had soon shattered it. Opening his account with a hook into the crowd, his 65 from 74 balls set the tone for the rest of the match, The tourists' batting matched their catching and by the close on day four they were almost 400 runs adrift with only five wickets in hand. Game over. The final coat of whitewash was applied at Port Elizabeth where, again, the South African innings began in a stylishly violent fashion. Having offered a desperately simple chance early in his innings that, inevitably, went down, Richards tried to right the injustice to the bowler by playing fast and loose with his wicket. The altruistic gesture misfired as he raced to 81 in no time. This spirit of inventive abandon was equally evident in his century that followed in the second innings, leading former Australian Test player Keith Miller – himself a legendarily rakish performer with the bat – to enthuse in a piece for the *Melbourne Sunday News*: 'True he was dropped thrice, but look at the style… it is great luck for me and the big crowds to see this new cricketing find in such brilliant mood.'

Richards and his colleagues had little time to bask in the glow of their glorious victory; their next engagement was a tour to England and some familiar dark clouds had started to gather. On 22 May the storm broke, as the Cricket Council announced that they would accede to the government's request to cancel the tour. The announcement represented a satisfactory end to a period of intense lobbying from Peter Hain's 'Stop the Seventy Tour' campaign. The South African Minister of Sport, Frank Waring, was less impressed, stating that the decision amounted to 'bowing down to irresponsible elements that manifest a total disregard for sport and the rights of others.' A somewhat ironic turn of phrase given the situation in his own country.

On a superficial level the hastily arranged series between England and a Rest of the World XI filled the gap that the cancellation left in that summer's programme of cricket. For Richards inclusion in this sideshow was no substitute: 'The contests never had the authentic atmosphere of a country-versus-country conflict; the heady emotions of our win against Australia remained firmly imprinted on my heart.' This in essence describes the sense of ennui that would, in time, overshadow his playing career. A glorious talent, tested and proven against the best, now yearned for a suitable stage. Like a thoroughbred stuck on the gallops, a Ferrari used for pootling down to the shops, Richards needed a clear run; the County Championship, Currie Cup, even World Series Cricket – it just wasn't the real thing.

By 1970 Coca-Cola was – having re-adopted the slogan from a back-catalogue including gems such as 1904's 'Coca-Cola is a delightful, palatable, healthful beverage' – and were willing to sponsor a talented young batsman to spend a season in Australia playing grade cricket with the Prospect club. The makers of the 'Friendliest drink on Earth' (1956) provided a car and a salary boosted by the promise of a dollar for every run. The money was soon rolling in. Selection for South Australia meant the chance to face a battery of world-class bowlers – just the kind of challenge to energise superior talents. Driven by the 'the gift of thirst' (1952), Richards spent the Australian summer of 1971 trying to satisfy an unquenchable desire for runs. A double century at Adelaide against the touring MCC was merely a prelude to the 'dream' that followed a few weeks later in Perth during the match with Western Australia, 356 glorious runs clubbed to all parts of the aptly named WACA. Further sizeable centuries followed to secure the Sheffield Shield for South Australia and for Richards a personal record – 1,538 runs at an average of 109 – that only Bradman had improved upon. This was not to mention a wealth of experience to draw on when he returned to Australia the following summer for the Test series. Or so he thought. On 2 April 1971 the South African government took a decision that would have made more sense the previous day. Their rejection of the South African Cricket Association's proposal to include two non-white players in the Test squad would ultimately ensure that there would be no tour to Australia, or anywhere else, for many years.

Summers of Discontent, the title chosen by Richards for the chapter of his autobiography dealing with the seasons spent in England, isolated from the challenges of top-flight cricket tells its own story. His account of this period alludes to issues of quantity and quality; the relentless slog of the seven-days-a-week county circuit soured an already bitter taste of loss. 'After participating in the winning of a Test series, every other cricket experience is an anticlimax.' Add to this the burden of expectation that inevitably follows a rare talent – 'If I scored a hundred, I had only achieved what was expected… If I got out for anything less, I had failed' – and you have a potent recipe for frustration. A frustration that would also be felt by others and even lead to the suggestion that he would sometimes toy with his gifts, unconvinced that the occasion was worthy of them. Of course Richards denies that this was ever the case; but who could him blame if it was? There's a well-known aphorism from the world of football punditry often used to welcome the luxurious talents of overseas players into the British game. Usually delivered by a former player perched on a sofa in a warm studio it goes something like this: 'Your silky, samba skills are all very well, but let's see how he copes with a bog of a pitch on a wet night in Macclesfield.' Surely this is missing the point. Most of us have, at some time, hoofed a football in an approximately pre-determined direction, or managed to lay part of a cricket bat on a moving cricket ball and been utterly delighted about it. But from our sporting idols we want something more and, quite rightly, so do they.

In any event, even if Richards was occasionally guilty of giving less than his best to the Hampshire cause, the record books do not betray him; his ten full seasons with the county yielded over 15,000 first-class runs at an average of over fifty. In selecting Richards as his batsman of the 1970s, Colin Cowdrey noted that where Boycott had made a virtue of discipline, the opener from South Africa 'has it all, and a flair for the big occasion.' Not unlike the man signed by Hampshire in

1971 to produce arguably the most mouth-watering opening pair that ever sauntered onto a cricket field. Where batting was concerned, Cuthbert Gordon Greenidge clearly shared a basic philosophy with his South African colleague: if it's there to be hit, hit it (hard). If the Bajan's first two seasons had yielded fairly modest results, his contribution to Hampshire's golden summer of 1973 revealed a talent that would, in coming years, make some of the world's finest bowlers look like mugs.

One would assume that, in mid-May, a soggy Leeds would not be the destination of choice for most opening batsmen. Greenidge begged to differ, busying himself by heaving the Yorkshire bowling attack to a variety of exotic locations both in and out of Headingley; he carried his bat to within one decent tonk of a double century. A century for the D.H. Robins' XI against the touring New Zealand side notwithstanding, Richards began his championship campaign in a more sedate fashion. At the Courtauld's Ground in Coventry he would move matters on, making the most of the short boundaries to smash a swift double century against a Warwickshire attack that included the raw pace (and wild hair) of a young Bob Willis. Having established their individual credentials, the openers then combined their talents. In the weeks that followed, Surrey, Lancashire and Worcestershire would all watch the scoreboard rattle past 200 before separating the pair. Ironically, the critical innings of the campaign owed more to careful ball-watching than crash, bang, wallop. Having been set a meagre target of 90 for victory by Northamptonshire, Hampshire's most likely rivals for the title, victory seemed a formality. Two factors suggested otherwise: the Southampton pitch was turning like a dervish trapped in a revolving door and the away side had the mercurial talents of Indian Test spinner Bishan Bedi at their disposal. Faced with a cricketing test worthy of the name, Richards nudged, prodded and only occasionally flayed his way to 37 match-winning runs in thirty overs.

On the last day of August Hampshire were confirmed as county champions for only the second time in their history. Sharing over 2,800 runs and 71 catches, the contribution of the openers had been decisive both in front of and behind the wickets. Had it not been for bad luck with injuries and the weather, further titles might have followed, particularly when the unpleasantly quick Andy Roberts arrived from Antigua, to complement the majestic mayhem instigated by the dream team at the top of the order. Hard work on Sunday afternoons during the blazing summer of 1975 did, however, produce another trophy. With 666 runs to his name, Boycott's form may have been devilishly good but Richards was supreme – the John Player League's star turn finished with 689.

Despite his leading role in a side that matched success with style, Richards could still feel his love of the game – never stronger than during that solitary Test hurrah – fading with every passing season. He had pitted his skills against the best, on the biggest stage, and now he was trapped in a piscine mixed metaphor – a big fish in a small pond, shooting fish in a barrel. Mike Procter, a teammate from the glorious rout of 1970 and fellow superstar of the English game during the decade that followed, recognised the rarity of the gift his friend possessed: 'If I had to pick one batsman to play for my life it would be Barry Richards. He was such a complete all-round batsman that if he felt like it, he could bat all day and the bowlers couldn't do a damn thing about it.' Quite how much Richards did feel like it, as the years rolled by, is open to question.

It is little wonder then that when, in sight of his tenth season in county cricket the chance of a final turn on the world stage came along, Richards seized it. The 'circus' tag often applied to Kerry Packer's World Series Cricket venture can be taken in two ways: a sneer from the establishment, disparaging its gaudy commercialism, or a literal description – the floodlights and outlandish costumes (who could forget the mighty West Indies in 'Coral Pink') – were certainly redolent of the Big Top atmosphere. Whatever your view of World Series Cricket, its brief life confirmed Barry Richards as a world-beater, graced with the talents to suit any occasion. If his double century in the fifth 'Super Test' in Perth showed the artist at work – an exhibition of shots and style to overshadow the centuries that followed from Greenidge and

Viv Richards – an unbeaten century to win the final at the Sydney Cricket Ground displayed the knowledge and skill of a craftsman.

'I know that when I walk off a county ground for the last time it will be with an enormous sense of relief,' Richards admitted in his autobiography. Published ten years after he first took to the field for Hampshire, at times the book makes for uncomfortable reading. It describes a rapid and eager ascent to the height of sporting achievement, followed by a protracted, rather laboured descent into frustration and, ultimately, despair. It is clear that, at times, these emotions were evident in his demeanour on the field. Richards' story may be clouded by the dud hand that fate played him but his contribution to the English domestic cricket scene is clear enough. Setting aside the runs scored, records broken and trophies won, he added something that is unquantifiable and beyond price in sport – entertainment. Like Compton and Miller before him and his namesake Viv in later years, Barry Richards was a crowd-pleaser, a dasher, an emptier of bars and no sport can ever have too many of those.

FOUR

RAGING BULL

It is 1981, the first Friday in July, and two brawny cricketers are departing the field of play. The captains of their respective teams, they are travelling in opposite directions and as they cross, something unseen passes between them – a mantle shifts. English cricket has a new raging bull. When South African all-rounder Mike Procter crossed the rope at Northampton's County Ground it signified a farewell to English cricket and to the team with which he had become literally synonymous, following more than a decade of heroic and dashing performances. The reception that greeted Ian Botham's return to the pavilion at Lord's – England were 1-0 down in the Ashes series and he had just scored a duck – was considerably cooler.

The events that followed his demotion as captain secured Botham's status as an icon of English sport. A great deal has been written and said about his visceral century in the following Test at Headingley – it is arguably cricket's 1966 – but, perhaps unsurprisingly, it was the television commentary of Richie Benaud that provided the most acute observation on the subject. As Botham scooped yet another ugly bouncer from the tip of his nose into the stand, Benaud remarked dryly that he was off to collect a copy of the latest edition of *Boy's Own*. This was indeed a sporting feast to appeal to our inner child. Delighting in the same suspension of disbelief that convinced us that Pelé had won the Second World War with a bicycle kick, Headingley 1981 offered an escape into the realms of pure fantasy. It was the kind of performance in which talent and temperament combined to brand a passage of sporting history with the imprimatur of an individual player at the top of their game; check the title of the commemorative DVD, the 1981 series was undoubtedly 'Botham's Ashes'. This same accolade applied to the man that Botham succeeded as the chief purveyor of *Boy's Own*-style heroics on the cricket field, for in the late 1960s and 1970s thrill-seeking fans headed for 'Proctershire'.

The Gloucestershire crowd caught their first real glimpse of the talents that would enthral them over the coming years during a tour match at Bristol in 1965. Eddie Barlow's South African side were threatening to overwhelm the West Country team when Procter and Barry Richards, two teenagers promoted from the Second XI, held their compatriots at bay with a century stand. It seemed that everyone was a winner that day, the two young bucks showed their mettle, the South African Test selectors caught a glimpse of a bright future and the crowd witnessed a compelling contest. Fortune would subsequently be more selective with her gifts. English cricket fans held their luck – Procter bowling to Richards would provide one of the great battles in county cricket for years to come – but the two young men who had dreamed of playing many more great innings together for their country, no doubt to this day, still have those dreams. In any event the promise they displayed during that match encouraged Gloucestershire to take a punt on the futures market. When the rules governing the employment of overseas players in the county game were relaxed three years later, they invested in Procter.

At the time his first season appeared prodigious; hindsight tells us that it merely represented par. Within the coming years he would achieve the double of 1,000 runs and 50 wickets more often than not. Had it not been for injury towards the latter part of the summer, Procter may well have found the extra 31 wickets he needed to secure membership of a most exclusive 'double' club; a club founded in 1874 by another useful Gloucestershire all-rounder, Dr William Gilbert Grace.

Never one to underestimate his own ability, Grace was the antithesis of the modern British sportsman who, possibly as a result of advances in media training, invariably comes across as a pretty cautious soul. We are all too familiar with their predilection for taking one game at a time, the inferiority complexes ('there are no easy games at this level – the Haitians are a useful side') and their rallying cry at the start of a new campaign, 'with any luck we'll be there or thereabouts come the end of the season'. Having secured sixteenth spot in a field of seventeen in 1968, it is a fairly safe bet that the Gloucestershire team that embarked on their quest for the County Championship the following season would have regarded finishing 'there or thereabouts' as a recklessly lofty ambition. Fortunately their overseas star had other ideas.

There is no doubt that 1969 was an Indian summer; monsoons in May gave way to baking heat that stretched into early autumn. Procter mastered the erratic elements and most of the batsmen who faced him; in claiming over 100 wickets at a cost of fifteen apiece he was, *Wisden* observed, 'the biggest single factor in the re-emergence of the county of Grace and Hammond as a power in the land.' Second only to an inspired Glamorgan side, the man with the 'ox-like shoulders' had hauled Gloucestershire from the foothills of the Championship to within sight of its summit. And so it came to pass; the golden bible blessed him as one of the cricketers of the year. 'The sight of Michael John Procter with his unruly straw-coloured thatch, sometimes kept in place by a bandeau, hurling down his expresses with an action almost defying exact analysis has become one of the most exciting spectacles of modern cricket.' An unorthodox, much-discussed action and a hair grip? Here was a sportsman way ahead of his time. In fact Procter's 'time' (and that of the other members of South Africa's golden generation) would come soon enough and then, with equal haste, disappear forever.

By the time that Procter arrived in Bristol for the 1970 season he was widely regarded as one of the foremost attacking bowlers in world cricket. The preceding series between South Africa and Australia had ushered some major young talents onto the world stage. The brutally stylish treatment to which Graeme Pollock and Barry Richards had subjected some pretty experienced Australian bowlers was complemented by the horrors that the new-ball partnership of Procter and Peter Pollock had visited upon their batsmen. Procter himself recognises the performances in what turned out to be his final Test series, as his zenith with the ball: 'To those who say I've bowled fast in county cricket, I say, "You should have seen me against Bill Lawry's side"'.

The English summer that followed brought mixed blessings. The 'Stop the Seventy Tour' campaign – which at its height saw Lord's shrouded in barbed wire – lived up to its name, denying players like Richards and Procter the chance to apply their local knowledge in the Springbok colours. Their consolation was selection, along with their national skipper Eddie Barlow and the Pollocks, for a Rest of the World team to take on England over five 'Tests'. For the home side, if taking on the world was not incentive enough, a collective eye was also straying Down Under towards the forthcoming Ashes series, there was form to be found and tour places to be won.

The winter of 1970/71 saw two batsmen with laughably diverse styles at the very top of their game. In Australia Geoffrey Boycott was immovable; combining a technique straight out of the MCC coaching manual with a bloody-mindedness straight out of Yorkshire, he batted for days, weeks and months until he was damned sure that England had regained the Ashes. Elsewhere in the southern hemisphere, Mike Procter, a man with a pleasantly straightforward take on the ancient and noble conflict between leather and willow – 'I like the idea of these blokes running up and bowling at me, while I try to thrash the ball out of their reach' – was also busy rewriting history. By the time that the Western Province wicketkeeper – the improbable-sounding Gavin Pfuhl – finally caught Procter during a Currie Cup match against Rhodesia in Salisbury, the big-hitting all-rounder had reached a personal record score of 254. More significantly he had completed a sequence of six successive centuries to join illustrious companions in the share of a world record. Don Bradman hit the magic half dozen for South Australia during a Sheffield Shield spree in 1938/39, while the legendary C.B. Fry finished a prolific first summer of the twentieth century with six of the best, completing the straight at Lord's

1. Divine intervention or sheer determination? Basil D'Oliveira's talent and perseverance earned him an escape from the uneven playing fields of apartheid South Africa...

2. ...yet it was in the more relaxed atmosphere of English cricket that he would face his sternest test.

3. A time to grovel: During the arid summer of 1976, the West Indies' thirst for revenge over Tony Greig was unquenchable.

4. Greig courts controversy again as Kerry Packer's World Series Cricket sends a tremor through the English sporting establishment.

5. Another day, another hundred: Barry Richards' genius was a double-edged sword: delight for followers of Hampshire, ultimately despair for the artist in search of a broader canvas.

6. Time gentlemen, please. Barry Richards and Gordon Greenidge – surely the most exhilarating opening pair ever seen in county cricket – step on to the field and the bars empty.

7 & 8. Capable of reducing opponents to jelly with both bat and ball, the all-round menace of Mike Procter carried Gloucestershire for well over a decade.

9. Ken McEwan's prodigious run-scoring helped push Essex to the summit of domestic cricket during the late seventies and early eighties.

10. Another middle-order powerhouse, Peter Kirsten aims high at Derbyshire.

11 & 12. *Opposite and right*: Captain Marvel. In both thought and deed, Clive Rice's leadership ensured that Nottinghamshire enjoyed the most successful period in their history under his stewardship.

13. Hair-raising! The Sussex new-ball attack of the early eighties was the stuff of fairytales: Imran Khan provided the beauty, Garth Le Roux was the beast.

14. In a single season of county cricket with Middlesex, Vintcent van der Bijl – the gentle giant from Natal – confirmed his status as a world-class bowler.

15. Allan Lamb in typically pugnacious form for Northants in the Benson & Hedges Cup final…

16. …and showing a more measured approach in India as England progress to an improbable series victory.

17. Left in limbo: Robin Smith's skill and courage against fast bowling was a defining feature of England's batting during the difficult journey from the eighties into the nineties.

18. Bubbles and troubles: The career of Graeme Hick at a glance – unparalleled success with Worcestershire...

19. …and struggling with lofty expectations (and lethal bowling) at Test level.

20. Taxi! Allan Donald sends yet another England batsman on his way.

21. Making giant strides: Having helped to establish Zimbabwe in international cricket, Andy Flower has since guided the progress of Essex and England.

22. In the balance: day five at the Oval in 2005 and Kevin Pietersen drops down on one knee; meanwhile, the nation sinks on to both, in silent prayer…

23. …and all rise and give thanks – the Ashes were to return to England, after eighteen long years. They would be gone again eighteen months later, despite the efforts of KP.

playing for the Rest of England against Yorkshire. Fry, who had already broken the world long-jump record, went on to earn his international soccer cap, appear in the FA Cup final and (he claimed) come within a whisker of the throne of Albania.

Procter took his regal form with the willow back to England the following summer, scoring seven centuries for Gloucestershire. Despite his remarkable consistency of performance across all disciplines of the game, the county continued to yo-yo wildly between the top and bottom of the Championship table. They celebrated a creditable runners-up spot in 1969 by plunging back down to seventeenth place the following year; by the end of the 1972 campaign they were riding high in third place. They were, in short, a punter's nightmare. The summer of 1971 proved an exception to the rule, neither battling for the title nor scrapping to avoid the wooden spoon, they achieved what has become the Holy Grail for most football clubs in the cash-sodden English Premiership – 'mid-table respectability.' As ever there was nothing mid-table or respectable about the way that M.J. Procter approached his cricket that year. It is ironic that a player steeped in the Corinthian ethic of the supremacy of the team over the individual would, through his own dashing brilliance and aggressive pursuit of unlikely victories, completely overshadow the efforts of his team-mates. Reading between the lines of his unequivocally titled

treatise on the game, *Mike Procter and Cricket*, one can sur-
mise that the coping mechanism he deployed to deal with
the loss of top-flight cricket was to try and inject urgency
and drama into every game he played through his style and
approach: 'All the really satisfying innings of my career have
been when the side has been up against it and we've had to
struggle through. Anyone of ability can get an easy 100 on a
flat wicket against a tired attack, but a batsman who gets his
side out of trouble has the double pleasure of personal and
team satisfaction.'

A classic exposition of the Procter doctrine lit up that
summer of 1971 during the Championship fixture with
Yorkshire at Bramall Lane. With Boycott's side monopolising
the first day to compile 225, declarations in the subsequent
two innings left Gloucestershire at tea on the final afternoon
with an unappetising victory target of 180 runs in less than
an hour and a half. Many on the county circuit would have
hoisted the white flag of pragmatism and blocked and prodded away for a draw; all Gloucestershire's raging bull saw was
a red rag fluttering in the distance. Boycott deployed spin
after the break looking to tease out indiscriminate shots –
they followed at such a rate from Procter's bat that the future
England pace bowler Chris Old was hastily recalled to the
attack to put the brakes on but to no avail. The big man from
Durban thundered on his merry way, slicing and carving the
bowling to all parts of the Blades' ground, finally coming to

rest at a match-winning III – unlucky for Yorkshire and one in the eye for the safety-first brigade.

Despite their Sisyphean progress towards the Championship title during the early 1970s, Proctershire were steadily evolving into a team, on their day, capable of giving any side a run for their money. Tangible results finally arrived in the form of the Gillette Cup in 1973, in which their leading man characteristically held back his bravura performances for the main stage. Man of the Match in the semi-final against Worcestershire, he followed a rapid century with three key wickets, that of a youthful Imran Khan among them. He repeated this successful formula in the final at Lord's, clubbing 94 in good time, and then restricting the Sussex response with some accurate bowling before nipping out two wickets at the death to secure the trophy.

With a month to go in his first season as skipper, Mike Procter decreed that his team, to a man, should hastily cultivate moustaches. This was not the work of a man giddied by power and the heat of the sun, rather that of an avid cricket historian. At the time of Procter's edict, Gloucestershire were closing in on a first Championship title since W.G. Grace had led the County to victory exactly 100 years earlier – and the previous class of '77 had been a hairy bunch. W.G. led from the front, of course, with a beard you could lose a small child in, his brothers G.F. and E.M. sported variations on the mutton chop and soup-strainer melange, while the rest of the lads

– with a selection of cavalry spurs, walruses and nailbrushes
– followed hirsute. It is often said that sport is won and lost
on the margins; whether the muzzies worn by Procter's men
could be classed as 'performance enhancing' is open to question – that modicum of extra weight keeping a batsman's
head down over a textbook cover drive, for example – what
we do know is that in 1977 Gloucestershire enjoyed one of
the finest seasons in their modern history.

Inevitably their messianic captain led by example. Though
at times during that summer he would run amok with the
bat, it is best remembered as the pick of his many fruitful
seasons in England with the cherry. His 109 wickets squeezed
out at only eighteen a piece represent his greatest haul for
an English summer; echoing the centenary, 1877 had seen
W.G. enjoy his best year with the ball, amassing 179 at a
very reasonable twelve runs each. But before the title race
had even begun to smoulder, Procter's team had already collected a trophy and their progress to the Benson & Hedges
Cup final was largely inspired by the skipper's ripsnorting
bowling form. His 3-15 dispatched Middlesex in the quarter-
final, while a stunning 6-13 against Hampshire in the semi
not only provided Procter with the satisfaction of a hat-trick
– his second of the season – but also the particular pleasure of including his erstwhile international teammate Barry
Richards within the trio. The final itself saw brain triumph
over brawn as Brian Brain overshadowed his skipper with

handy figures of 3-9 as part of a great all-round performance in the field by the West Country side.

For Gloucestershire their early season success reversed the old culinary cliché beloved of football managers – the cup was the icing on the cake, now they needed to focus on the bread and butter of the league. As July turned into August, a run of three straight victories hinted at the possibility of a glorious centenary celebration – it was time to stop shaving. The run began at Cheltenham where Procter single-handedly battered Worcestershire into the turf. His 7-35 in the first innings restricted their opening gambit to 167; a century batting at no.7 then set-up a useful lead and 6-38 sent them home with a whimper, all out for 136. Success against Sussex and Hampshire followed, but two draws and a defeat thereafter meant that Gloucestershire needed to beat Glamorgan in their penultimate fixture to keep apace with title rivals Kent and Middlesex, as they headed down the home straight.

Their victory at Sophia Gardens owed much to Procter's skill as a bowler and his tenacity as a captain. Taking 5-56 in Glamorgan's first innings to leave them 150 runs adrift, he then declared Gloucestershire's second innings at only 18-1 to give his bowlers the time, if not the runs, to seek out a victory. In the event it was child's play, Glamorgan capitulated as John Childs (another headline writer's dream) took five wickets and Procter himself accounted for four. And so the Championship would come down to the last round of games.

It is ironic that the very thing that had given impetus to Gloucestershire's season – the bullish, brilliance of their leader – may, arguably, have led to their fall at the final fence. Procter's honest appraisal of his captaincy in that last match suggests that his natural instincts overcame his better judgement: 'Looking back I think I made a tactical error by not playing it tight enough. I was so totally convinced that we were going to win that game that I attacked in the field all the time.' For the first three innings of the game Procter's instinct, and form, looked spot on. He began with a century, took 6-68 and then added a half century to leave Hampshire with 271 to find on the final afternoon. It seemed an improbable target; sadly for Gloucestershire the man who led the chase, Gordon Greenidge, spent much of his career making the improbable look effortless. The match, and the Championship, were lost.

During Procter's remaining years with the county they would never again threaten to add to Grace's last triumph but his individual heroics would continue to thrill the crowds irrespective of their allegiance. In 1978 over 1,600 runs and 69 wickets were enough to earn him the Wetherall Trophy as the leading all-rounder in first-class cricket – a prize of some value in the era of Botham, Imran and Hadlee. The following summer his superhuman exploits owed more to Marvel than *Boys Own*, demonstrating in some style Procter's mantra: 'The bowlers should be the nervous ones as they run up to bowl at you – they should be thinking, "God where's he going to smash this one?"' In the summer of 1979 the answer to this question was simple – everywhere. The mayhem began in earnest during August as he hammered the Leicestershire bowling attack for a century before lunch, before putting their batsmen to the sword with figures of 7-26. This onslaught with the ball included a hat-trick, a turn he repeated in the next match against Yorkshire. Like Ali naming the round in which he would fell an opponent, Procter then declared his intention to hit the fastest century of the summer, in one of the four remaining games. He slugged a ton in seventy-six minutes against Surrey, then battered his way into the nineties against Somerset and Warwickshire in forty-six and thirty-five minutes respectively. He left it late but, as ever, delivered: in his final knock of the campaign, Procter caned the Northamptonshire bowling to all parts of the County Ground in Bristol, reaching a century in only fifty-seven minutes and making good his promise to secure the 1977 Walter Lawrence Trophy.

My earliest cricket memory is Headingley in 1981. Before then I had formed a composite image of the model professional from the greying MCC posters adorning the walls of the school cricket pavilion: caps, pressed flannels, Brylcreem, the odd pipe, textbook defensive shots, jolly good show – Botham shattered all that. This great bearded oaf, grinning in the face of hopeless odds as the ball whistled towards his forehead he slogged it into a baying crowd – for a nine-year-old gaping open-mouthed at the TV, this was sporting perfection, a maverick genius who knew no fear. Or so I had thought. In *Botham's Century*, his look back at the finest players of the past 100 years, he sheepishly confesses to having once stepped back towards square leg to escape a vicious bouncer. 'Somerset were playing Gloucestershire on the day I had to walk out and face this South African maelstrom and, for the first and last time in my career, or for that matter, my life, lost my bottle.' The bowler in question was of course, Michael John Procter.

FIVE

ADOPTED SONS

Writer, philosopher, explorer, fisherman, the mythological Chinese luminary Fu Hsi was such a promising all-rounder it is safe to assume that if he had been around in the mid-1980s, rather than the twenty-ninth-century BC, he would have been hailed as the 'next Botham'. Better known as the original author of the *I Ching*, an ambitious first stab at making sense of the cosmos, I prefer to think of Fu as a pioneer in the field of sports psychology. When applied to the business of getting results on the pitch, who can better his theory of the dynamic balance of opposites – the Yin and Yang dichotomy? Take rugby union, for example: in the 1990s the British Lions found the perfect centre pairing, combining a big lump, Scott Gibbs, to punch holes in the defence, with the grace and pace of Jerry Guscott to dart through them. Or what about the unstoppable Liverpool team of the early 1970s? Toshack and Keegan's little-and-large show was irresistible. Cricket is no different, where partnerships can make a team and break an opponent. Many former English Test batsmen, no doubt, still lie awake at night reliving the twin horrors of Glenn McGrath's bounce and nagging line at one end, and Shane Warne's relentless guile and variation at the other. I'm sure that their colleagues from the bowling department suffer with similar memories of trying to break up the Waugh twins. Mark, the elegant stylist stroking the ball all over the park, Steve the flinty, immovable rock. Following the same principle, if South Africa had needed to recruit a middle order duo of contrasting yet complementary styles for a Test cricket team during the late 1970s and early 1980s they would have needed to look no further than the English counties – the trusted firm of McEwan and Kirsten had offices in Essex and Derbyshire.

Ken McEwan first displayed his talents in England during the summer of 1972, playing for the Sussex Second XI following a recommendation by Tony Greig. Although the young man made a favourable impression, amassing runs with verve and style, the places allotted to overseas players down on the South Coast were already taken. But the following year, in the unlikely setting of North Inch in Perthshire, the man from Bedford, Cape Province, turned in a performance for Essex against Scotland that would secure his employment for the next ten years and usher in a period of unprecedented success for his new masters.

With two solid seasons of acclimatisation and steady progress under his belt at Essex, a near 2,000 first-class runs in 1977 established McEwan as a prodigious and powerful middle-order batsman, while the following summer a string of stellar performances earned him the ultimate stamp of approval in the English game – a nomination as one of the *Wisden* cricketers of the year. Like two of his co-nominees, Ian Botham and Bob Willis, McEwan enjoyed success that year against both domestic and visiting opposition. With Botham straining at the leash, an eager novice in the international arena, and Willis, rampaging his way to a century of Test wickets, both men left their mark on Greg Chappell's Australians as England romped to a 3-0 Ashes victory. McEwan's weapon of choice was the bat, which he wielded with rapier-like precision but also such force that the ball sang to the boundary as if thumped there by a cudgel. The unbeaten century he collected off the tourists at Chelmsford in midsummer signalled the start of a red-hot streak. It began with a Sunday League century against Warwickshire on the final Sunday in June. The following day he gave Sussex an extended view of the talents they had let slip by carting their bowling attack, Greig included, all over the park for a glorious double century. He then remounted his assault on the Bears, with twin Championship centuries at Edgbaston, before travelling to Southend to smash yet another century, in this instance against Gloucestershire. Striding out of the pavilion for his second innings, with five successive tons behind him, McEwan must have felt unstoppable. Seconds later he was making the return journey – the central victim in a Mike Procter hat-trick.

McEwan's personal successes in his early years in England would soon be matched by the collective achievements of his team; between 1979 and 1985 he was a key member of an Essex side that swept all before them, collecting eight major trophies. A versatile outfit with strengths in all areas of the game, they could play it fast and loose – three Sunday League titles, a NatWest trophy and four Benson & Hedges finals proved that – or summon up the guile and skills needed to succeed in the longer contests. The nouveau riche of the county circuit – the wealth of talent at Yorkshire, Lancashire and Surrey had historically hogged the silverware and dom-inated the thoughts of the England Test selectors – during the 1980s Essex came to the party in style. In fact, between 1979 and 1993 the battle of the sexes turned the County Championship into a duopoly, with Essex and Middlesex sharing eleven of the fifteen titles. It was the former that laid down the first marker in 1979, running away with the Championship by seventy-six points to complete a league and cup double, following their earlier success against Surrey in the Benson & Hedges Cup final. Having announced their arrival with such force, the Essex side that would dominate the English cricketing landscape for many years to come now had the confidence to match their all-round talent. A shrewd captain, Keith Fletcher, was blessed with a group of players capable of delivering a valuable sporting oxymoron, consistent variety. At the top of the order a youthful Graham Gooch provided a solid platform ahead of the blazing strokeplay of McEwan and the Scottish grit of Brian Hardie in the middle order. In the bowling department the left-arm swing of John Lever always kept batsman guessing until the last moment, while Ray East was a first-class spinner and world-class comedian. If humour is the glue that bonds a group of individuals into a team, then East was the Araldite in the Essex dressing room. There was a subtle anarchy about his antics that transcended the mere Deep-Heat-in-the-jockstrap approach to sporting japery – imagine Gazza scripted by Peter Cooke. He once borrowed a bicycle from a spectator to make the journey from point to square leg between overs; on another occasion he responded to a dubious decision before lunch by returning to the crease after the break, with bat and pads to explain to a startled umpire, 'But I thought you were joking.'

Despite this occasional buffoonery, Fletcher's men were rapidly becoming serious contenders for all of the major competitions. In 1981 they collected their first Sunday League title, with McEwan topscoring, and two years later, when they reclaimed their County Championship, the South African was again the leading batsman – indeed he would finish the summer caught between the sublime and the meticulous: just behind Viv Richard in the averages, just ahead of Geoffrey Boycott as the season's most prolific run-scorer. The race to that year's Championship went down to the proverbial wire and, with over 2,000 runs to his name, McEwan's contribution was a key factor in Essex's last-gasp triumph over Middlesex. In more ways than one it was a victory stamped 'made in South Africa'. Aside from McEwan's thumping form, the 98 wickets contributed by Lever and the 1,000-odd runs added by Graham Gooch may not have been forthcoming had they had the distraction of Test cricket that summer. Their participation in a rebel tour to South Africa the previous year and subsequent three-year ban by the TCCB ensured that Essex had their full attention.

The three international exiles combined their talents again the following year to cram yet more silverware into the Essex trophy cabinet. Another Sunday League title was secured with relative ease but the Championship was another story. With almost 4,000 runs between them, Gooch and McEwan again led the way with the bat; Lever was just as important and added a century of wickets. Even then, heading into the closing weeks of the season, it was Nottinghamshire that had their noses in front thanks to the all-round performances of their thoroughbred Richard Hadlee, who completed the magic double of 1,000 runs and 100 wickets during the campaign. In the end the title race came down to the final play. At Taunton, Nottinghamshire's last-wicket pair needed to find four runs for victory from two balls. Keen no doubt to avoid the place in tabloid history that his surname demanded, Mike Bore, opting for a dramatic finish, gave the penultimate ball a mighty heave-ho and was caught a few yards inside the rope.

The next season, McEwan's last in England, followed the pattern of those that had preceded it, with Essex mounting strong challenges on all fronts. Although their quest for a third successive Championship title would ultimately fail – Middlesex took the honours that year – their form in the limited-overs competitions was peerless. But for a below-par performance in the Benson & Hedges final, they might have claimed a cup treble. They returned to Lord's in September to face Nottinghamshire in the NatWest Trophy final – the only title missing from the hoard collected since the first success in 1979. Seemingly impervious to a bowling attack spearheaded by Richard Hadlee, the opening pair of Gooch and Hardie provided a dream start with a double-century stand, allowing McEwan free rein to come in and blast away merrily until the close. Although the Nottinghamshire openers Robinson and Broad, who were both vying to partner Gooch atop the England batting card, responded with a century stand, the wickets kept tumbling, pushing the victory target ever further away. Only Derek Randall held firm and, with one over to go and twenty runs needed for victory, set about his task with gusto, biffing the ball around HQ to bring his side to within two runs of victory. At this point he went for one final slog and was caught, allowing Essex to scrape home by a single run and complete their full set of trophies.

Four years earlier, a similarly dramatic dénouement to the NatWest Trophy final had signalled a milestone of sorts for another English county. By sneaking a run from the final ball to match Northamptonshire's score, Derbyshire claimed the honours by virtue of having lost fewer wickets, ending a trophy drought stretching back to their Championship campaign of 1936. In many ways the final was won and lost in the southern hemisphere; the efforts of two South Africans and a Kiwi turned the game. When Allan Lamb, the powerhouse of the Northants middle order (who would go on to play a decade of Test cricket for England), was run out in single figures, it signaled the start of a batting collapse. A century stand from the New Zealand Test player John Wright and Peter Kirsten – who, conversely, would wait another ten years to play for his country – set-up Derbyshire's scramble for the line.

The trophy represented a reward for a county side that, although lacking the strength within the squad to sustain a challenge in the Championship, had developed into an effective unit in the one-day competitions. To a certain extent, this tenacity was honed during the mid-to-late 1970s under the captaincy of Eddie Barlow, one of the stars of the South African Test side that had played its last competitive match in 1970, it was then adopted by England players Geoff Miller and Mike Hendrick and the imported talents of Kirsten and

Wright. Although the latter pair shared two attributes, the mental and physical energy needed to play a long innings, and a protein-rich diet (thanks to the cut-price meat supplied by Vic Cooper, the butcher from whom they rented their digs), their batting styles were quite distinct. Wright was solid and orthodox, a lamb chop with potatoes and two veg, Kirsten was more like a chicken vindaloo, possessing a sizzling array of shots his wristy style and brilliance against spin brought a taste of the subcontinent to the East Midlands. When he was hot, he was on fire.

Kirsten's propensity for putting together unbeatable winning streaks first came to the fore in South Africa during the 1976/77 Currie Cup when, playing for Western Province, he rattled up scores of 173, 103, 107, 165, 22, 111 and 128 in consecutive innings. Back in England, opposing captains and their bowlers would soon learn that if they let Kirsten settle, he would destroy them. In the summer of 1980 he would score three double centuries before the end of June and finish the season as the highest run-scorer in first-class cricket – only one decent knock short of the elusive 2,000 run mark; it was a landmark that, at the time, only Donald Carr had achieved for Derbyshire. Aside from his record return during the 1959 season, Carr, a great servant of the county both on the pitch and in the committee room, secures a further entry in cricket history as the first man to lead an MCC tour to Pakistan that threatened to cause a diplomatic incident.

Long before Mike Gatting wagged an accusatory finger at Shakoor Rana, Carr's tour of 1955/56 erupted into mayhem when, one evening after dinner, a group of England players – engaged in what the MCC later referred to as high-spirited 'ragging' – upended a bucket of water over Idris Begh, one of the local umpires standing in the match.

The following year saw Kirsten lead the Derbyshire first-class batting averages and the scoring in their successful NatWest Trophy campaign. It was, however, the summer of 1982, his last in England as a county player, that was his most prolific as he embarked upon another white-hot streak of form, clattering five centuries in five matches in July, culminating with an unbeaten brace of hundreds against Surrey. Only Warwickshire's diminutive Guyanese genius Alvin Kallicharranan scored more first-class runs that year and with John Wright adding 1,830 to Kirsten's haul of 1,941, one wonders what Derbyshire might have achieved with a bowling attack to match the meaty strokeplay of their leading batsmen.

A brilliant fielder and more than useful bowler, the only thing that Kirsten did not have on his side was time. After his spell in England was over he would have to wait almost a decade to pull on a shirt bearing the Protea. By then it was a slightly tighter fit than it would have been during his heyday, when a fleet-footed, dashing young batsman had cut a swathe through the English bowling attacks of the mid-1980s. That said, the experienced elder statesmen provided a useful foil for the young guns that emerged to help ease South Africa back into the international cricket fold. One such rising star was his younger half-brother Gary, who was in his early twenties when South Africa returned and would go on to play 101 Tests and break numerous batting records. However, for many commentators Peter's was the greater talent; Milton was right, chance governs all. In 1994 the brothers travelled to England with Kepler Wessels's side, the first official party their country had sent since 1965. The three-match series exemplified the character of the two sides, South Africa were dogged, tenacious and consistent; England were at times brilliant, at times hopeless. The latter came to the fore in the first Test, as South Africa confirmed the old adage of touring sides always raising their game at Lord's by batting well twice, then skittling their hosts out for a pitiful 99 to win the game.

The drawn second Test at Headingley was notable for two batting performances. The first belonged to Mike Atherton, a characteristically belligerent innings of 99 raised two fingers to the media critics that had gathered following the so-called 'dirt in the pocket' incident during the previous Test. The other significant knock at Leeds came from Peter Kirsten; batting in conditions usually referred to as 'typically English' he scored a century of composure and class to steady a South African innings that was on the slide and earned himself the Man of the Match award in the process.

The historic series ended with honours even as England came back to win at The Oval, thanks largely to Fanie de Villiers. It was his short-pitched delivery that nailed Devon Malcolm squarely on the badge of his helmet, sending him sprawling to the floor. When he got up he was cross, very cross, and famously announced: 'You guys are history.' Too often a maddeningly unpredictable performer, Malcolm made good on this promise, unleashing merry hell on the South African batsmen to finish with figures of 9-57, thus squaring the series.

Like many described in this book, the playing careers of Messrs McEwan and Kirsten are shot through with 'ifs', 'buts' and unanswerable questions. If a South African Test side had toured England a decade earlier than they eventually did the pair would have made for an irresistible middle-order combination – powerful hitting complemented by elegance and finesse. But if they had been preoccupied with Test cricket, would they have been able to contribute their skills and energies so wholeheartedly to the task of transforming their respective adopted counties into genuine contenders? When batting their timing was impeccable, in historical terms it was way off. Missing the Test cricket boat at both ends – too young in the 1960s, too old in the 1990s – they did at least perform in the domestic game at a time when the regular contributions of Test players from England and other nations gave the competition a keen edge. Rather than look for answers, it is perhaps simpler to accept the critical role played by fate in the life of any professional sportsman. Let's give the final word to Confucius, another great sports psychologist way ahead of this time: 'The wheel of fortune turns round incessantly, and who can say to himself, I shall today be uppermost.'

SIX

LEADING BY EXAMPLE

Having simmered for two Tests, the infamous Bodyline series of 1932/33 finally boiled over at Adelaide, when a short-pitched delivery from Harold Larwood caught the Australian batsman Bert Oldfield just above the right eyebrow, dropping him lifelessly to the turf. At Oldfield's subsequent funeral, Larwood accepted the role of pall bearer. Happily for all concerned the two events were over forty years apart – the skull-fracturing bouncer cementing a friendship that would endure long after their playing careers had finished. The story goes that England skipper Douglas Jardine first hatched his controversial strategy for reclaiming the Ashes shortly after completing an innings for Surrey against Nottinghamshire as he sat in the dressing room admiring the colourful assortment of bruises that the pace attack of Larwood and Bill Voce had recently pummelled onto his torso. By the late 1970s the Trent Bridge coconut shy was back in business, now under the control of foreign owners, but producing similar results. With their differing styles – Richard Hadlee offered incisive precision, Clive Rice muscular aggression – the Kiwi–Springbok partnership soon became the scourge of visiting batsman.

These days, with the international cricket calendar bulging at the seams, Test players performing at the top of their game have become a lesser-spotted breed on the domestic scene. Thirty years ago the situation was quite different. Fans of world-class all-rounders could feast their eyes on the talents of Procter, Imran and Botham. At Trent Bridge it was pure gluttony, as in the decade between 1977 and 1987 Rice and Hadlee collected the Wetherall Award – presented by the Cricket Society to the leading all-rounder in English first-class cricket – no fewer than seven times between them. Befitting a Nottinghamshire cult hero, Rice had many strings to his bow – strike bowler, middle-order batsman, athletic fielder – but perhaps his greatest impact was as the captain that led Nottinghamshire to two Championship titles and pushed them to the forefront of the domestic game during his tenure.

Awarded his county cap in 1975, the man from the Transvaal had soon established himself as a model of consistency in never dipping below the 1,000-run mark with the bat, rarely straying above an average in the twenties with the ball. Within four seasons he had been installed as skipper and instantly ran into trouble. Like many of his compatriots pacing the annual treadmill of county and provincial cricket, Rice yearned for a shot at the big time and a chance to perform on the international stage. As a youngster, earmarked for a bright future with the Springbok side, he had stood on the threshold of the Test cricket arena, just as the door was slammed shut. A patient man, he was still there twenty years later when it creaked ajar, to lead his country on their first adventure after the long years of isolation.

In 1979 it was the ever-present spectre of World Series Cricket that cast the darkest shadow over his nascent career as leader of the Nottinghamshire side. Having established and maintained a party line on the subject of Packer's venture, the Trent Bridge establishment reacted sharply to the involvement of their star player, stripping him of the captaincy and even pressing for his removal from the playing staff. As with many of the contretemps spawned by World Series Cricket, lawyers would soon be circling overhead. Following a reconciliation of sorts, Rice maintained his place in the side but the reins of leadership were handed back to his predecessor Mike Smedley. The South African's continued excellence with bat and ball and obvious aptitude for leadership soon made a mockery of this political fudge – as *Wisden* observed: 'Above all else Rice, like so many Springboks, is dedicated to winning… Whether with the bat, the ball or in the field, he has consistently produced the kind of performances that have uplifted less talented colleagues.'

By 1980 he was back at the helm, steering Nottinghamshire to third place in the County Championship – their best showing for over half a century – and achieving personal honours in the shape of a nomination from the golden bible as one of the five cricketers of the year. For some, Nottinghamshire's creditable and perhaps unexpected ascent may have signalled a period of consolidation but Rice, bound by the southern-hemisphere ethos that views second place as 'first loser', had other ideas. His Wetherall Award for the following summer recognised a superb double of almost 1,500 runs at 56, and 65 wickets at less than 20. Nottinghamshire's coronation as champions that year – ahead of Sussex by two points – owed much to his ability to motivate a side to play at its peak and fight to the bitter end of a campaign. As Mike Brearley, arguably the ultimate thinking cricketers' captain, observed that year in an essay for *Wisden*: 'There are teams which would need an exceptionally bad captain to prevent them from winning, while others could be led by Napoleon and still be doomed.' Rice clearly knew how to get the best from his troops. Building a team on the clichéd but solid principle of blending youth with experience, he managed the sublime genius of Hadlee, coaxed the whimsical best from Derek Randall and nurtured the diverse talents of men such as Eddie Hemmings, Tim Robinson and Bruce French onto the international stage.

As skipper and match-winning all-rounder, Rice was ideally placed to lead by example. Any side that snatches its first

Championship title for decades in a race so close that the final points margin falls at 304-302 will, at times, be compelled to ally mental toughness with the requisite skills. Midway through that historic season, during their away tie with Hampshire, the captain delivered a masterclass in the art of keeping your head while all about you are in danger of losing theirs. Literally. The venue was Dean Park in Bournemouth and in conditions favouring the ball the home side unleashed the ultimate weapon, Malcolm Marshall. The brilliant Bajan who would spend much of the 1980s breaking the hearts and bones of English batsman, was running amok. With the exception of Rice the only batsman that made double figures was Robinson and he only reached 10. The sight of their captain progressing serenely to an unbeaten 105 out of a total of 143, as all hell broke loose around him, would be a source of inspiration for the others as the season gradually played out to its tense finale.

This ability to produce an optimum level of performance when the conditions were at their most challenging was a characteristic that Rice shared with many of his compatriots that left their mark on English cricket. Like D'Oliveira, Procter and Greig, he prospered when the stakes and expectation levels were high. As *Wisden* observed: 'There is something of the showman in his make-up, being often at his best when a ground is full and he can respond to the sort of crowd participation upon which he would thrive if the

Test door were open to him.' Interesting choice of words, if playing Test cricket for South Africa was not an option, what about England? In the early 1980s Allan Lamb and Chris Smith were making the smooth transition from overseas stars to homegrown talent. Ironically the unavailability at that time of certain England players – banned following the 1982 rebel tour to South Africa – meant that the selectors were grateful for an expanded pool of talent to call upon. It cannot have escaped their attention that a Test side boasting an engine room manned by Botham and Rice would take some stopping. In the event, the South African all-rounder resisted the temptation. When the rebels toured his homeland in the guise of the South African Breweries England XI – with Boycott and Gooch opening, a pub side only in name – Rice was there, but as a loyal member of the opposition. A regular fixture in various select world sides during this period, he was happy to beat his England colleagues, but drew the line at joining them.

In 1987 he did, however, turn out in the bacon-and-egg stripes of the MCC to help them celebrate their bicentenary with a match against the Rest of the World. Yet even in the more relaxed atmosphere of exhibition cricket, the old bedfellows of controversy and South African sport sought each other out. Having broken Martin Crowe's hand during the match between Somerset and Nottinghamshire some weeks earlier, Rice had accepted the invitation to replace the Kiwi batsman on the MCC XI. Seventeen years after Lord's had needed the protection of barbed wire against the perceived threat of angry dissent, a nostalgic sense of panic descending on HQ following his selection. In fact the occasion did not produce any controversy and with a fearsome battery of world-class bowlers in front of him, Rice determined to seize the moment: 'Put it this way, there was no way they were going to get me out, it was as simple as that. It was a fantastic opportunity for me and I couldn't wait to show off my skills.' This he did, repelling the advances of Imran Khan, Kapil Dev and a youthful Courtney Walsh to score an unbeaten half century and even top Roger Harper's astonishing 'run out and bowled' dismissal of Gooch to claim the award for the outstanding fielder in the match.

But for Rice, the MCC festivities that year were merely a temporary distraction from the serious business at hand, pushing Nottinghamshire towards success in the domestic competitions. As followers of the English Premiership will attest, a league comprising twenty-odd sides that perennially slides into a two-horse race can become a rather tedious spectacle. Following their unexpected success in securing the 1981 County Championship, Nottinghamshire were determined to maintain the pressure on the big two – fourth behind Middlesex in 1982, second and fourth behind Essex in 1984 and 1986 – until Rice's final summer at Trent Bridge in 1987, the county secured another title to complete the cycle of success that had begun with his reinstatement as captain at the turn of the decade. But it was a close-run thing. By late summer the title looked like it might be heading for Old Trafford, as Lancashire powered towards the finish line. Heading into the final round of games, Nottinghamshire needed a decisive performance against Glamorgan to set a stiff target for their Lancastrian rivals.

In his last Championship appearance at Trent Bridge, the captain signed off in style with two vital wickets and a pair of sharp catches in the Glamorgan first innings saw the visitors skittled out for 111; his unbeaten century led the reply that effectively closed off the game. Although Lancashire rounded off their campaign with victory over Essex at Chelmsford, they remained four points adrift with the bonus points earned in that crucial last round of games proving decisive. The confirmation of Nottinghamshire as Championship winners also secured their status as double winners – the NatWest Trophy had gone their way the previous week thanks, perhaps inevitably, to crucial contributions by Rice and Hadlee.

Ten years after he had bowed out of county cricket, the keen eye that had served Clive Rice faithfully during his playing career glimpsed something that would shape the future of English Test cricket. The occasion was Nuffield Week – the annual play-off for the leading school teams in South African cricket – and the eye-catching performances were delivered by a young man playing for Maritzburg College, a young man called Kevin.

Some years later, when Rice learned that Kevin Pietersen – disillusioned by the lack of opportunities in his homeland attributed, somewhat controversially, to the racial quota protocols – was looking for employment in the English game. he moved swiftly to secure the youngster's signature on a four-year contract with Nottinghamshire. As far as English cricket is concerned, the rest is history.

SEVEN

CHARGING IN

W hen, in the summer of 1970, a lobbying campaign ensured that a group of Springbok players would not travel to play cricket on these shores, its organisers could hardly have imagined that ten years later, four of the five players honoured by *Wisden* for their impact on the English domestic season would have strong South African connections. For the record, an Australian completed the quintet. The simple fact is that as the 1970s gave way to the 1980s, the County Championship – the jewel in the crown of English domestic cricket – seemed, more often than not, to be falling into or out of African hands. In 1979 the bat of Ken McEwan powered Essex towards the first in a long series of titles. The following year their arch rivals Middlesex claimed the honours on the back of the hoard of wickets gathered by Vintcent van der Bijl. In 1981 the all-round skills and leadership of Clive Rice helped Nottinghamshire to edge past a

Sussex side inspired by the aggressive pace bowling of Garth Le Roux.

Following a series of rampaging displays that earned Western Province the Currie Cup in 1977/78 – 53 wickets at less than 15 speaks for itself – Le Roux had been drafted into the World XI squad for the first season of World Series Cricket. Emerging into the limelight from the shadows cast by stars such as Lillee, Garner, and Procter, the young fast bowler's nine-wicket haul in the 'Grand Final' pushed him into the centre of the stage. Whether they liked it or loathed it, few in the cricketing world could ignore Packer's glitzy farrago; an eye-catching performance on that platform guaranteed international exposure and potential opportunities for future employment. Months after his barnstorming display at the Sydney Cricket Ground, Le Roux was charging in at the slightly less glamorous County Ground at Hove – a trial of sorts against the touring New Zealanders – following another recommendation by Tony Greig, then in his last days at Sussex. Perhaps struggling with the alien conditions, Le Roux made little impact, taking a single wicket at the cost of over 100 runs. But with two more productive summers in the Cape behind him, he returned to the English south coast for a prolonged and successful stay. At Sussex he would join another imported talent to form a pace attack that was to become the stuff of fairytales. Imran Khan's languid style and elegant deceptions provided the beauty, Le Roux, snarling behind a drooping moustache as he unleashed a volley of aggressive, often short-pitched, thunderbolts was, of course, the beast.

The Sussex side that he joined in 1980 also boasted further South African talent in the form of Ian Greig, brother of Tony, and Kepler Wessels. The cricketing odyssey of Wessels – a Marlon Bando lookalike from the Free State – saw him play in the Australian Test side during the mid-1980s, before retuning to England in the twilight of his career as captain of the first South African tour there for almost thirty years. His last memorable act as a Sussex player was to smash the highest score of the season – 254 out of a 550 follow-on total – at Hove to earn a draw against the eventual County champions Middlesex. In the same innings, a clubbed fifty from Le Roux would also prove to be his final act of the summer as injury ended his season prematurely. When he returned in 1981 his form was inspirational. In a summer of spectacular comebacks – Botham and Willis defied their critics and hopeless odds to turn the Ashes series around, while at Wimbledon John McEnroe sought and gained revenge over Bjorn Borg for defeat in their epic dual the previous year – Le Roux achieved the impossible: he overshadowed Imran as the darling of the Hove crowd, leading the attack with 81 first-class wickets at less than 20 apiece. As the early weeks of summer were washed away by torrential rain, it was July before the Championship table began to take on any meaningful shape.

With the sun on his back, Le Roux eased into form, starting at Taunton with a ten-wicket haul to secure victory against Somerset, dethroning King Viv in each innings. The improving weather clearly agreed with another West Indian West Countryman, Joel Garner, who hit the magic ten-wicket mark on four occasions during the summer; a foretaste of the carnage he would wreak with his international colleagues on their tour to England three years later. Only one bowler took more wickets than Big Bird over the course of the summer, and they would prove decisive. Richard Hadlee's remarkable collection of 105 led the contributions from a strong and varied Nottinghamshire attack, while the runs of Rice and Randall provided the mainstay of the batting.

By the time that Imran and Le Roux had bowled Sussex to victory over Yorkshire at Hove during the final round of matches in mid-September, the title already belonged to the East Midlands. Following this brief flirtation with major success, Sussex would wait another twenty-two years before finally achieving the first County Championship title in their 164-year history. Proving the multiple buses theory, two more have followed in rapid succession, thanks in no small part to the wristy genius of their Pakistani spinner Mushtaq Ahmed and the runs of Murray Goodwin, a Zimbabwean Test batsman who opted for premature international retirement following his country's troubled tour to England in 2000.

Back in the early 1980s a touring party carrying even weightier political baggage was heading for the airport. The side described at the time by *The Daily Mirror* as, 'Gooch's Dirty Dozen' and vilified by Labour MP Gerald Kaufmann for 'selling themselves for blood-covered Krugerrands', touched down in South Africa in the spring of 1982 to play three four-day games and two limited-over matches under the banner of the South African Breweries English XI. This would be the second consecutive English cricketing winter that had borne the stamp of South African sporting controversy. The 1980/81 tour of the West Indies is famous for two things. First is the cancellation of the Second Test after the Guyanese government revoked the visa granted to Robin Jackman, objecting to the Surrey bowler's links to South Africa; he had previously spent several English winters coaching there. Second there was the 'over of the century' delivered by Michael Holding to Geoffrey Boycott in the third Test at the Kensington Oval. Six screamers culminating in a classic cartwheeling-stump denoument. The over described by the great sports writer Frank Keating as 'the hateful half-dozen' foretold most eloquently of the horrors that would be visited upon English batsmen by their West Indian brethren over the coming decade.

Although Gooch captained the rebels – becoming the focal point of political and press vitriol – it was Boycott, his opening partner in the Breweries side, who had been the key figure in the organisation of the tour. Like many in the party, Boycott had recognised that the prime years of his international career had passed; the players knew that sanctions in the form of bans from Test cricket were possible, but the risk was a calculated one. A lengthy ban seemed unlikely, and the financial rewards on offer for a winter sojourn in the African sun were not insignificant.

After a summer of Lillee and Thomson had followed the bombardment of the previous winter at the hands of Holding et al, England's opening pair could have been forgiven for assuming that, in the more relaxed atmosphere of an unofficial series, they would find some respite. Not so. As the first 'Test' got underway on a baked, bouncy deck at the New Wanderers Stadium in Johannesburg, the home XI wheeled out the perfect pair to give any batsman an early wake-up call. At one end you had Le Roux, built like the proverbial rustic latrine, bristling with bullish aggression. At the other, the damnation was sent down from the heavens; at 6ft 7in Vintcent van der Bijl was purpose built for slamming the ball down into the turf from on high and not to mention at great velocity.

The English batsmen had faced both men in the past, for Le Roux was midway through his successful tenure at Sussex, while van der Bijl's time in England had come and gone. He had played a single, yet spectacularly productive, season for Middlesex. However, these encounters had been in the more predictable environment of county cricket. Now their tormentors were charging in with a partisan crowd baying them on, hungry to exploit a rare tilt at international-calibre opposition.

It takes a special kind of player to achieve immortal status at a club in a single season – Jürgen Klinsmann's redemptive season in English football with Tottenham Hotpsur in 1994 offers a recent, rare example – but during his single summer at Middlesex in 1980, van der Bijl, the giant from Cape Town, acquired the rare dual status of legend and cult figure. The former stems from his immense contribution to a hugely successful campaign; the latter owes more to his striking appearance – a gleaming bald pate crowned his massive frame – and the attitude he took onto the pitch. *Wisden* described him as 'a breath of fresh air with his immense enthusiasm, his love of playing cricket, and his bubbling friendship for other cricketers.' While he had spent most of the 1970s shattering bowling records playing for Natal and Transvaal, unlike many of his contemporaries he had not sought employment with an English county. It may be hard to imagine in the modern globalised market for sporting talent, where money buys mobility, but van der Bijl resisted the urge to seek potentially lucrative situations outside South Africa to safeguard his primary source of income and security. A teacher by profession – that alarm bell you can hear chiming softly does indeed warn of approaching cliché – Vince certainly taught the batsmen on the county circuit a thing or two during the summer of 1980.

He was also fortunate to play his only season in English cricket in a team led by a man who would, soon enough, write his own chapter in the history of English cricket.

The year before he would achieve his greatest feat as a captain – arriving midway through a dismal Ashes campaign to cajole, inspire and condition a beaten group of players into an insuperable unit – Mike Brearley had faced a stiff challenge in the domestic arena. During the 1979 campaign Middlesex had fallen from their lofty perch above the chasing pack and landed in its midst. Fourteenth place in the Championship was not acceptable for a county that had become accustomed to being a contender for the title. In reality, the recruitment of a bowler whom Brearley would honour at the season's end as 'the biggest single factor behind our success', was, in many ways, a glorious mistake. Middlesex had assumed that their Barbadian destroyer Wayne Daniel would be unavailable for domestic duty, following selection for the West Indies side to face England in the Test series, leaving them light in the fast-bowling department. Thus the call to van der Bijl. When it transpired that the tourists had decided to muddle along with the likes of Marshall, Holding, Garner and Croft, the county was left with an embarrassment of riches.

The embarrassment they had suffered the previous year referred solely to their final position in the Championship. With his professional pride at stake, the 1980 season provided Brearley with a chance to put things right. A talented batsman and reliable slipper, his greatest gift lay, of course, in the art of leadership. Having stepped off the treadmill of domestic cricket in favour of more academic pursuits – taking a two-year sabbatical from Middlesex earlier in his career – his primary cause for return was the offer of the captaincy. A burden Brearley felt both necessary and rewarding, as he explained in an essay for *Wisden*: 'At times, the thought of letting someone else deal with the hassles is attractive, but however good it would be for my soul to give up the reins, I doubt if I could do so willingly and still play.' On a more pragmatic level he must also have recognised that the nucleus of a side good enough to win back-to-back Championships in 1976 and 1977 remained, and that subsequent arrivals and discoveries strengthened his hand. In the summer of 1980 the Middlesex dressing room bulged with players of international calibre. The bowling department was fully staffed in each of the main disciplines: Daniel and van der Bijl had the pace, Simon Hughes and Mike Selvey offered movement and variation, while John Emburey and Phil Edmonds both bowled spin for their country; the batting line-up combined experience with youth.

But they were not to have things all their own way. Across London at The Oval, Surrey had assembled a squad which, if not as blessed with star names, looked more than capable of finding the county their first Championship title since 1971. While Brearley would later acknowledge the importance of the wickets taken by his gangling South African strike bowler, the man who most helped Surrey to push their neighbours all the way in the title race was cast from a quite different physical mould. Built for brawling and with a nickname to match, Robin Jackman ('the Shoreditch Sparrow') nailed 121 first-class victims during the campaign. One of the four players with South African connections named by *Wisden* amongst their five men of the season (van der Bijl, Rice and Lamb were the others) it was Jackman's prodigious summer that propelled him into the consciousness of the England selectors and ultimately led to the controversy over the scheduled stop in Guyana, during the winter tour.

The first few summers of the 1980s saw a subtle shift in the cricketing relationship between England and South Africa. As the realisation dawned that the latter had no easy route back into international cricket, some difficult decisions had to be made. For the group of South African players turning in stellar performances in the English domestic game their frustration at the lack of a sterner test was understandable. Meanwhile the selectors for the English Test side, desperately combing the counties for another Botham, Gower or Willis, could not help but notice the wealth of talent unclaimed by any other nation sitting under their noses. When a group of current Test players were cast into the wilderness for three years following the rebel tour of 1982, the temptation on both sides to take a long, hard look at the qualification rules for 'non-English' players became too hard to resist. But those that did cross the Rubicon were carrying bats – Allan Lamb, the Smith brothers – sailing into a Caribbean storm of short-pitched mayhem that would characterise England's struggles during the remainder of the decade. One can only speculate, albeit idly, at how a side able to call upon a new-ball pair such as Le Roux and van der Bijl may have carried the fight just a few steps further.

EIGHT

DODGING BULLETS

To see the West Indian fast bowlers in action during the summer of 1984 was to witness poetry in motion. For the English batsmen on the receiving end, the words of Emily Dickinson no doubt sprang to mind: 'If I feel physically as if the top of my head were taken off, I know that is poetry.' The series began horribly and went rapidly downhill. On the first morning of the first Test, Warwickshire's Andy Lloyd celebrated his international debut in front of his home crowd at Edgbaston by ducking into a bouncer from Malcolm Marshall and out went the lights. Of the various indices used to measure success or failure on the sports field – best, worst, first, last – perhaps the cruellest is the consignment of an individual player to that special register of the archive marked: 'Answer to a pub quiz question.' Later that day, as he lay propped on a bank of hospital pillows watching a small squadron of tiny, tweeting birds circling his head, Lloyd no doubt hoped for a full recovery and swift return to the Test side. Sadly, neither came to pass. The permanent legacy of that blow to the temple was a 30 per cent impairment of vision in his right eye which, while not sufficient to end his county career, did mean that he never scored enough runs subsequently to break back into the England team. He spent precisely thirty-three minutes at the pinnacle of his chosen sport and, as any saloon bar genius will tell you, remains the only Test opener never to have been dismissed.

In his analysis of modern fast bowling, *Letting Rip* (the cover of which incidentally shows a semi-conscious Lloyd sinking to the turf), the journalist Simon Wilde catalogues every injury inflicted on batsmen by each of the Test-playing countries between 1974 and 1994. Wilde notes that the combined firepower of Australia, England, New Zealand, Pakistan, India and Sri Lanka contributed a total of forty-nine cases of actual and grievous bodily harm during this period. The West Indies alone were responsible for forty, seven of which bore the signature of their leading personal-injury specialist, the Barbadian Express, Malcolm Denzil Marshall. Even amongst the bowlers who have taken more than 350 Test wickets (an elite club of fifteen members at the time of writing), Marshall stands out. There are two particularly telling statistics: his average of 20.94 is the lowest on the list and his strike rate of a wicket every 46.7 balls is bettered only by the aptly named

Pakistani destroyer, Waqar Younis. Simply put, no batsman ever enjoyed a degree of comfort when facing Marshall.

Perhaps more than any other player, he seemed to epitomise the gulf in talent and confidence separating the two sides in the summer of 1984 – never more so than during the Headingley Test. It was here that he unexpectedly sauntered down the pavilion steps, ostensibly to escort Larry Gomes to a nearby century, with his left hand and wrist encased in a garish pink cast. Sporting only a faintly ludicrous, floppy angler's hat for cranial protection, he promptly slapped a ball from England's quick bowler Paul Allott to the fence one-handed. With the cast still in place, he then gutted the English order taking seven wickets (including a caught and bowled for pity's sake) for a mere fifty-three runs.

Having watched those boys of '84 in action, the debate as to which was the greatest ever Test team: the Bradman-led tourists of 1948, or Steve Waugh's record-breaking class of 2001 is, for me, a non-starter. Apart from the odd excerpt of *Pathé* footage, I never saw the former in action; I have, however, had ample opportunity to witness the genesis of the current Australian team – through the Border–Taylor–Waugh–Ponting axis – into a Test-match-winning machine, more often than not at the expense of England. Highly effective, ruthlessly efficient, good at what they do? Oh yes. The greatest? Not for me.

For the benefit of any Australian readers, this is not the knee-jerk reaction of a 'whingeing Pom' to twenty-odd years of Ashes drubbings. The simple truth is that when it comes to feasting my eyes on the sporting talents of others, my greed can only be truly sated if the hefty dollops of proficiency on display come with a generous side order of genius. And I'm not alone. During the 1970s and 1980s who did snooker fans vote the 'People's Champion'? Was it: a) 'Steady' Eddie Charlton? b) Cliff 'The Grinder' Thorburn? or c) Steve 'The Nugget' Davis, whose metronomic cueing action and judicious safety play earned him six world titles in nine golden years? The answer of course is d) none of the above. The title belonged to Alex Higgins, who blew a hurricane of booze, birds and brawls into the tabloids, and new life into what had previously been seen as a sport with limited public appeal. It was largely thanks to the volatile talents of Higgins and his natural successor, Jimmy White, that during the 1980s many of us were – as Chaz and Dave so pithily observed – 'Snooker Loopy'. And let's be honest, who was it that truly lit up Wimbledon? Pistol Pete Sampras, coolly shooting down opponents with his unerring serve and volley game, or McEnroe, dancing about the court on a knife edge, ready to blow his lid at the drop of a hat? On that basis, while I admire fully the gritty obduracy of a Steve Waugh and the immutable line of a Glenn McGrath, it's somehow not enough. Give me Viv Richards champing his gum insouciantly, as cool as the red, green and gold tricolour on his Rasta sweatbands, shuffling across his stumps to redirect a good-length ball from its middle pole trajectory onto the roof of the hotdog stand behind the pavilion. That is what I wish to see, and I make no apology for it.

With various batmen tried in various positions during that demoralising summer, perhaps the only consistent features of the English top order were the prolific belligerence of Allan Lamb and the ghastly run of form endured by the captain and leading talent David Gower. It is hard to imagine two players with more contrasting styles at the crease. Lamb crouched into a show of stocky pugnacity, chin raised in defiance at the bowler, moustache dancing wildly to the tune of rapidly chewed gum, backside jutting aggressively towards square leg. Gower, tall and languid, relaxed and still, a few golden curls straying below the line of his batting helmet, a strangely uncertain, almost vulnerable expression greeting the onrushing bowler.

That summer the pair even missed the ball in a markedly different fashion. As the West Indian quicks teased with searing outswing outside off stump, Lamb would aim wild, baseball-style scythes at the elusive ball, while Gower wafted a series of glorious cover drives through clean, fresh air. This laconic style both at the crease and as the team leader was not always to everyone's taste; following hefty maulings by the West Indies the media would often blame Gower's laissez-faire approach to practice and preparation. The more measured, almost militaristic regime favoured by his successors, Mike Gatting and, particularly, Graham Gooch, marked the contrast. Similarly, the elegant left-hander's bacchanalian tendencies – most professional cricketers acquire their nickname by appending 'o', 'y' or 'ers' to their surname, Gower's derived from the name of his favourite wine bar – would often lead to the kind of high jinks certain to elicit a frown of consternation from the Lord's establishment. His most infamous wheeze – arsing about in a vintage biplane during the Ashes tour of 1990/91 – sunk a nail deep into the coffin that would soon house his prematurely dead Test career. But history will add perspective to his tenure as skipper. Yes there were the hidings dished out by the West Indies – the clean sweep of 1984 was followed eighteen months later by another 5-0 drubbing, a phenomenon identified at the time by a media yet to discover political correctness as a 'blackwash' – but notable successes against others. Indeed, the two series that split the Caribbean carnage saw him lead the side to two historic achievements – victory in India and the reclamation of the Ashes.

Lamb headed for the subcontinent in rampant form. His simple philosophy during the summer – 'I decided after the first Test that there was no point in ducking and diving, because the bullet with your name on was never far away, so I decided to take them on,' his autobiography explains – had paid dividends. He had finished the summer with a fourth century during the one-off Test against Sri Lanka, to add to the backs-to-the-wall trio he had wrested from the West

Indies. With the rebel players still exiled his status as a senior tourist was enhanced. And so, when news of the assassination of Indira Gandhi broke shortly after the England team's arrival in Delhi, thus plunging the city into dangerous turmoil, it was Lamb who argued for the cancellation of the tour to safeguard the players. Following a robust exchange of views with tour manager Tony Brown, Lamb was ready to walk away from the tour. Gower intervened and brokered a peace between players and management but the tour from hell had only just started. On the eve of the first Test in Bombay, news reached the camp that Percy Norris, the British Deputy High Commissioner, who had hosted a reception for the players the previous evening, had been shot dead. The debate concerning the continuation of the tour now raged through both the camp and the media.

When it was finally determined that the game must go on, England's defeat by eight wickets was perhaps unsurprising. Less predictable was the recovery staged by the tourists over the course of the five-Test series, culminating in a resounding victory in Madras that would ultimately earn them the rubber. If captaining the England side to victory in India secured Gower's membership of a select club – only Jardine and Greig had managed this feat before – the fact that he did so after falling behind must make him its president. Factor in the incendiary backdrop against which the series was played and the result is even more impressive.

Gower's golden year continued into the English summer; Australia were visiting and recent Ashes history was on his side. The last two series had gone the way of the host team and England had every reason to expect the trend to continue; the new heroes of the Indian campaign would be joined by the return of some more familiar idols. Gooch appeared later in the summer to strengthen the batting, having served out his penance for the rebel tour and Botham, looking ever more the English lion – grinning under a shocking mane shot through with blonde highlights – returned as the Ashes talisman.

The Australians had fewer reasons to be cheerful. The batting strength provided by the Chappell brothers in the 1970s would not be replicated fully until the Waugh twins picked up the baton in the 1990s. As for the bowling, the potency of old was lacking: Lillee had recently called time on his career and Thomson's unexpected swansong late in the series proved that his best had passed some time ago. The series still had to be won – a draw would leave the urn in Australian hands – and as six Tests were played out over a long summer, England gradually pressed home their advantage. With the top-order powerhouse of Gooch and Gower often providing the platform, the middle order of Lamb, Gatting and Botham enjoyed the freedom to drive a forceful and aggressive second wave, avoiding that most particular English failing, the middle-order collapse.

Flushed with their success against India and Australia, the English bandwagon rolled on to the Caribbean where, instantly and inevitably, the wheels fell off. Gatting left the party early, beaned by a Marshall bouncer that smeared his nose across his face and blacked both eyes, Lamb failed to recreate his dashing form of the previous encounter and Gower's tour was epitomised by the anthem boomed out of ghetto blasters around the Islands throughout the series: 'Captain, your ship is sinking.' By the end of the English season that followed it was wrecked irreparably, dashed on the rocks of an Indian side that no one had expected to beat England at home. Between his two encounters with India, Gower's captaincy stock had risen and plunged; the reins were handed to Mike Gatting to lead the side to face the summer's second tour by New Zealand.

Dropped for the first two Tests and returning at The Oval only to make a duck, Lamb's international career was now facing its first significant crisis. The way that he played and approached the game, the risk of failure was an unavoidable possibility. To describe him as 'hit and miss' would perhaps be unfair to his technique and talent, but a glance at his series-on-series record betrays a failing that he shared with the curly haired girl in the nursery rhyme: his form – that most elusive and indefinable sporting phenomenon – was either very good or horrid. He found himself increasingly in the latter camp following his contribution to the Ashes recovery of 1985. While he clung to his place long enough to enjoy the successful defence of 1986/87, as part of the team led by Mike Gatting, an average below twenty saw him omitted from the troubled home and away fixtures against Pakistan that followed.

Edged to the background of the Test picture, he was still a central feature of England's one-day landscape. Although at the time the evolution of strategic thinking had not fully embraced the concept of the short-game specialist, Lamb clearly fitted the bill. His middle-order pragmatism was ideally suited to guiding an innings to a successful conclusion – whether setting or chasing a target he could accumulate or dominate as the situation required. As ever the numbers tell the story, his average of 36 in Tests places him squarely within a group of middle-order contemporaries who never quite achieved the level of consistency in Test cricket that view forty as good, fifty as excellent. The demands and pace of one-day cricket lowers this bar a notch; here Lamb's average of 39.32 is mere decimal places below an upper echelon reached by only a handful of England players.

In view of their recent history in the tournament, it seems fanciful to imagine England reaching the denouement of three World Cups. But in the 1987 competition hosted by India and Pakistan, with Lamb leading the averages, they literally swept their way to a second final – on the spin-friendly pitches it was the safest and most profitable shot in the bag.

Once there, Mike Gatting added another blot to a copybook that would, within the year, be a filthy mess, by misjudging a reverse sweep off Border's part-time spin to hand victory to the Australians.

Returning to England to face the West Indies the following summer, the skipper would soon have more to worry about than the prospect of another nasty biff on the bugle. Having led the side in the drawn first Test – a win in all but name in light of the pastings that had gone before – Gatting suddenly found himself at the centre of a very English crisis, following tabloid allegations of nookie with a barmaid in a hotel in Leicestershire. Although the TCCB appeared to accept his explanation of the incident, the dismissal that followed perhaps owed more to their lingering distaste at Gatting's shouting match with umpire Shakoor Rana in Faisalabad during the previous winter's tour to Pakistan, and their resentment at the frank tone of his autobiography, *Leading from the Front*. In the spring of 1990, disillusioned with his treatment at their hands, Gatting would raise a pair of digits in the general direction of the English cricketing establishment in a time-honoured tradition by leading a rebel tour to South Africa.

As one career stalled, another shuddered back into life. In the same way that he had first proved his worth, Lamb used a home series against West Indian firepower to re-establish his credentials. But despite his efforts in the rearguard, the results were dispiritingly familiar, as the remaining four Tests went the way of the visitors. Although on the face of it a 4-0 reversal may not appear to signify giant strides, it did represent a turning point of sorts. The stranglehold that the West Indian golden generation had held over England since the 'grovel' series of 1976 was finally loosening. Throughout the 1980s and early 1990s, a procession of kings of the willow – Lloyd, Greenidge, Haynes, Richards – would abdicate leaving a solitary prince called Brian to rule in their place. The passage of time would also bring respite for batsmen around the world from the storm whipped up by a production line of lightning-fast bowlers. Walsh and Ambrose kept the flame burning up to the turn of the century, but their back-up was rarely in the same class. This emerging shift in the powerbase underpinning world cricket would soon become apparent to England as their next two series saw them join battle with the once and future kings.

The pretenders to the throne arrived in England in the summer of 1989 determined to rise from the ashes of their recent failures. Following consecutive defeats at home and away, the side led by Allan Border was, by design, a tougher nut to crack. Sensing that familiarity with the enemy would dull the keenness of their competitive edge, the captain steered his players away from the matey, let's-all-have-a-beer-together-afterwards culture evident in previous encounters. This grittier, professional ethic was personified by a man who would, during the summer, embed himself like a thorn into

English flesh and remain there for over a decade, Stephen Rodger Waugh. It was Waugh that set the tone for the series – thankless toil for England, ruthless Australian dominance – with an epic century in each of the first two Tests. A cool, implacable figure at the crease, his gunslinger eyes watching the ball race to the boundary, Waugh was a walking signpost pointing out an Ashes future full of English suffering and Australian triumph. The first Test in Yorkshire was just chapter one. The new chair of selectors had thrown the bar of soap that was the captaincy back to Gower and he, perhaps anticipating an esoteric performance from the Headingley pitch to assist his all-seam attack, put the Australians in. On the third day with their hunger for runs finally sated, the tourists declared at 601/7; Waugh's unbeaten 177 provided the foundation stone for the innings. Following his dashing 102 from 104 balls in the one day game at Trent Bridge, Lamb was the in-form man and led the home response with a measured century. Once England had avoided the follow-on and the Australians had batted for a second time, a draw looked inevitable as the game entered its final day. That was until Alderman skittled England out for 191. Lamb's contribution to a miserable summer for English cricket ended there – shortly after the Test he aggravated an old shoulder injury originally sustained during a lemon-throwing contest with Gower and was out for the duration. England's tragi-comic relationship with the Ashes had begun in earnest.

The tour to the Caribbean that followed the foreboding 4-0 defeat at the hands of Australia started in the most dramatic and unpredictable fashion, England won. Catching their hosts cold at Sabina Park, the tourists took their first Test off the West Indies since 1974. The bowlers set up the sting, knocking over a batting line-up that still included the likes of Greenidge, Haynes, Richards and Richardson for 164. The batsman, led by Lamb's century, inhaled the rare sniff of victory deeply and outperformed their illustrious opponents to win by nine wickets. With the hex finally lifted the tourists continued their resurgence in the third Test – the second was lost to rain – and looked set to chase down their victory target until some dilatory tactics from the fielding side secured the draw as the gloom closed in on the final session.

The West Indies reasserted themselves, winning the next Test at Barbados despite another gritty century from Lamb, captaining England for the first time in the absence of the injured Gooch. With the series level and the weight of history pressing down upon him, the stand-in captain took his side to Antigua for the final match with everything to play for. After successive hammerings over the preceding decade, Lamb knew that the spoils of war would be rich; immortality beckoned for the captain that could win, or even draw, a series against the West Indies on their home turf. He also knew that his troops, with Gooch sidelined and Gatting and Botham at home, were short on experience, especially amongst the batsmen. It was time to call up the cavalry. With Gower in the Caribbean working as a journalist, Lamb lobbied hard for his inclusion but Gooch – whose relationship with the stylish left-hander became increasingly fractious as their careers played out – and tour manager Micky Stewart were set against the plan. With England's most talented batsman looking on from the press box, Lamb's men were cut apart by Ambrose, Bishop and Walsh, lost the match by an innings and the series with it.

By the turn of the decade, England were looking to follow Australia's example and adopt a more focussed, professional approach to the game and, as with any revolution, there were casualties. The regimented approach that characterised Gooch's captaincy, with its emphasis on fitness and hard work, contrasted starkly with the more laid-back approach of some of the previous regimes. Returning to the side in the summer of 1990, Gower seemed to personify the old guard – relying on instinct and natural ability over the rigours of circuit training. As Gooch's vice-captain and a card-carrying member of the beer and skittles club, Lamb was now treading a fine line. At least on the field he left little room for doubt, with two centuries in a mini-series with India, including a strong supporting role at Lord's as Gooch compiled his epic 333, secured his place and held at bay the claims pressed by younger men.

The following winter, midway through another Ashes spanking, the tensions simmering gently in the camp suddenly came to the boil over an incident that threw the differences between the two senior men and most important players in the team into sharp relief. For Gooch, the best way to motivate a teammate struggling for form was through coaching and practice; for Gower the logical remedy was to commandeer a Second World War biplane and swoop low over the ground on which they were batting. *Chaq'un a son gout.* The infamous Tiger Moth incident splintered the already brittle relations within the party; Lamb's intercessions on Gower's behalf edged the vice-captain closer to the door of the tent.

His form during the English summer that followed did little to reassure the selectors. For once underperforming against his favourite opponents, a return of 88 runs from seven innings against the West Indies was patently inadequate. His selection for the winter tour Down Under owed more to reputation and experience than form; three Tests against New Zealand would preface the World Cup and Lamb's knowledge and skill in the middle order of the one-day side were still too valuable to discard. Unlike the last three tournaments – at the time of writing Australia have just sewn up a hat-trick of titles without wasting a bead of sweat – the fifth World Cup presented no blindingly obvious favourites. Perhaps stifled by the expectation levels rising from the home soil, Australia had a shocker, losing far too many games in the opening round to qualify for the latter stages. England, spurred on by a rejuvenated Ian Botham – reborn as an opening bat in the kind of pinch-hitting role that the Sri Lankans deployed to devastating effect in the subsequent tournament – would reach the final. The team they would ultimately face in the 1992 showpiece had staggered rather than sprinted to the final – they were skittled out by England for just 74 in the first round, before losing to über-rivals India – and at various points looked dead and buried. Their charismatic captain had other ideas, encapsulating the spirit that drove them on in his famous exhortation as the bell rang for the last round: 'The motto of the day is play like a cornered tiger.' The team was Pakistan, their captain was Imran Khan and both would have a role to play in the controversies that characterised the closing acts of Lamb's playing career.

When the new World Champions travelled to England the following summer for a Test and one-day series, they arrived with more baggage than most. On the cricket field the two nations shared a recent history littered with ill-feeling and, at times, open confrontation. The ugly tableau depicting the nadir of this period – the famous shot from the 1987/88 tour of the furious finger-wagging duel between Mike Gatting and Shakoor Rana – articulates the prevailing mood better than any words. The series played out a decade earlier had also, at times, danced on a knife edge, not least as a result of the fanatical appealing that provided the soundtrack to the maddening, leg-spinning genius of Abdul Qadir. That summer had been Lamb's first in international cricket and his run of scores against Pakistan – 6, 5, 33, 0, 0 and 4 – had plunged his top-flight future back into immediate doubt after an impressive start in the earlier matches against India. This malaise continued throughout his Test career – a blot on his statistical copybook, he averaged just over twelve in his encounters with Pakistan – and would indirectly bring it to a close.

The sequence of events that saw Lamb suspended and fined by his county, fined by the TCCB and required to defend and then pursue two separate libel actions in the High Court, began at Lord's, during the fourth game in the one-day series. The Test matches played out earlier in the summer had raised all too familiar tensions, driven to a large degree by the defining and decisive feature of the series – the art of reverse-swing bowling. There are various factors that can cause a cricket ball to swing as it travels through the air, but the main culprits are God and man. The former may provide the necessary forces of nature – humid conditions, heavy cloud-cover – the latter can address his attentions to the ball itself, as far as the law allows. The substance of the complaint brought by Lamb was that the Pakistan bowlers had crossed a line drawn by Law 42(3). Following his intervention, the umpires changed the ball during the lunch break and there the incident might have rested. However, when subsequent official media releases stated that the ball had been changed because it was out of shape – with no reference to any infringement – Lamb decided to go public. The interview he gave to *The Daily Mirror* effectively ended his England career – unauthorised statements to the press constituted a breach of his contract with the TCCB – and the subsequent hearing and appeal drove a wedge between the player and the cricketing establishment. His comments also warmed the ears of former colleagues and adversaries. Later that summer, walking through the Long Room at Lord's, following a net ahead of the NatWest Trophy final, he was served with a writ. Sarfraz Nawaz, a former Pakistani Test bowler who had played with Lamb at Northants, took issue with a reference in *The Daily Mirror* article to Sarfraz's alleged knowledge of the darker arts of swing bowling. The claim was eventually withdrawn, but not before the door of the High Court had been passed. The saga reopened at the same venue in 1996 when Lamb joined Botham in an unsuccessful libel action against Imran for comments directed towards them in an article for *India Today*.

With his international career behind him, Lamb was able to dedicate himself fully to his county duties. From his arrival in the summer of 1978 to his swansong season of 1995, his contribution to Northants, a side from outside the traditional strongholds, was consistent and significant; an average of over fifty from 256 first-class matches tells its own story. His captaincy of the side over seven seasons mirrored his style with the bat in hand, impulsive, often impetuous, and rarely afraid to gamble. Like many of his compatriots that found their way into English cricket, he would occasionally catch the mutterings of dissent and discontent at the style, approach and, inevitably at times, failure of this foreign import. The irony that underlay the sporting politics of the time were rarely more evident than during his first summer as an England player, when English colleagues in the Northants dressing room – Peter Willey and Wayne Larkins – languished on the sidelines, exiled from Test cricket after their part in Gooch's rebel tour. In his final year with the county he assumed the mantle of a potentate, adding the roles of manager and coach to his captaincy duties. *Wisden* editor Matthew Engel described a figure 'strutting round the county grounds like Napoleon', who led the side to a creditable third place in the Championship and luckless losers in the NatWest Trophy final.

To properly evaluate Lamb's career, one has to step back and look at the wider context in which it was set; he played through a period of transition. The amateur era of boozy mischief and greater fraternisation between the players gave way to a harder, sharper, more professional ethic; on the pitch the mantle of walloping England was gradually passed from the West Indies to the Aussies. Blessed with few serious injuries but too often cursed by form that oscillated between the sublime and the ridiculous, Lamb's decade-long residence in England's middle order vexed elements of both the cricketing establishment and the media. To an extent he was a beneficiary of circumstance – the bans that followed the two rebel tours removed potential competitors for his place – but he also chose his allies well, staying close to the more gregarious and influential characters in the side. Often criticised for playing fast and loose too early in an innings, the same aggressive and combative style was also a valuable asset to an England team that all too often found itself on the back foot, under heavy fire. Like Greig, whose footsteps he followed into both the England captaincy and the High Court, and Basil D'Oliveira, he tended to produce his best form when the deck was aflame and the ship listing dangerously.

NINE

THE CON ARTIST

During the glorious summer of 2005 the headline, 'England Pick Flipper at Last' carried a simple meaning: the English top order were finally emerging out of the web of deceit spun around them so beautifully for more than a decade by Shane Warne. In February 1921 the same banner told an entirely different story. Losing 3-0 to the Old Enemy and the Ashes gone, a bold throw of the English selectorial dice was needed to rescue some pride. A. Dolphin was called into the side to keep wicket in the Melbourne Test. Sadly the experiment proved unsuccessful and was never repeated, but Arthur Dolphin went on to play a further seven seasons for Yorkshire and, of course, frolic happily in the shallows of sporting trivia for eternity. By contrast, the arrival of Warne in the English summer of 1993 prefaced a long and eventful stay at the heart of international cricket that would, perhaps inevitably, also foreshorten the careers of many opponents.

When Robin Smith walked out to bat on the second day of that's summer Old Trafford Test, the look of stunned disbelief frozen on Mike Gatting's face as he passed him on his way back to the pavilion – the proud recipient of the 'Ball of the Century' – was simply a warning of the torment that was to follow.

Having displayed the appetite and technique for fast bowling that had also characterised the early Test career of his compatriot Allan Lamb, Smith of Hampshire via Natal suffered more than most with the twists and turns of the spinning ball. A relatively undemonstrative character off the pitch, once he stepped on to it with a bat in his hand he became a riot of aggressive motion. A man for whom self-belief and confidence were capricious bedfellows rather than long-term partners, this transformation was a crucial part of the preparation process. His talent had never been in any doubt – as a schoolboy he had broken Barry Richards's batting records – the uncertainty lay in finding the belief and faith in his ability to face the challenges presented by top-flight cricket. His older brother Chris, a key figure in helping Robin develop from youthful prodigy to reliable Test performer, was eager to see Robin capitalise on the chances that had passed too rapidly during his own career.

Chris had arrived in Wales at the tail end of the 1970s to play for Glamorgan but was poached swiftly by Hampshire soon after he had smashed a century off their bowlers

during a Second XI fixture. The South Coast club were looking to plug the gaping hole left at the top of their order when
the brilliant Gordon Greenidge left for duty with the West
Indies. This temporary arrangement lasted over a decade as
Chris became a mainstay of the Hampshire order but, early
on in his stay, to his long-term cost, he was seen as the answer
to the question burning at the heart of English cricket during the early 1980s – where have all the openers gone?

As the two central figures in the first of the rebel tours
to South Africa in the spring of 1982, Geoffrey Boycott and
Graham Gooch – who scored over 17,000 Test runs between
them – had effectively ruled themselves out of Test selection for the next three years. Although Boycott's strokeplay
would enliven the county circuit for some years to come,
his Test career had run its course. One only has to look at
the contribution made by Gooch to the overall solidity and
competence of England's top order, following his subsequent
rehabilitation during the 1985 Ashes campaign, to appreciate
the size of the hole left by his exclusion.

The selectors attempted to hammer various square pegs
into the void during that period. Kent's Chris Tavaré, for
example, whose debonair moustache and exotic, accent-
laden surname promised a flashing blade wielded with stylish
Gallic abandon. *Au contraire.* With profound apologies to
Chris, he was – at least whenever I was watching – the dull-
est batsman on the planet. His infuriating habit of strolling

towards square leg after every ball, as if considering in some depth how to deal with the next delivery, only to return to the crease to execute yet another judicious block made him something of a *bête noire* amongst the pre-pubescent set that had seen the light during Botham's Headingley slog-fest in 1981. It was noticeable in school matches at this time that any batsman showing the slightest tendency towards a defensive approach was instantly heckled from the boundary with a nasally groaned chorus of 'Tavaraaaay! Tavaraaaaaay!'

Another understudy keeping Gooch's crease warm was Lancashire's Graham 'Foxy' Fowler. As a regular guest of the BBC Test Match Special commentary team, Foxy is often berated for being a southpaw play-and-miss specialist, a poor man's David Gower, and a purveyor of numerous woolly woofs outside off-stump, unmatched by a sufficient number of classical cuts and drives. This verdict seems a tad harsh, with a little more luck, Fowler might have enjoyed an extended run in the Test team. A well-established member of the side due to face the Australians in the home series of 1985, he aggravated an injury in training that, it was subsequently discovered, dated back to a car crash from 1979. He not only missed that series but never played for England again. On the plus side, he was involved in one of the most astonishing English batting performances in history. Having watched our batsmen being ground into the dust by the trident of Marshall, Holding and Garner during the summer of 1984, my expectations for the tour to India the following winter were not excessive. Imagine my surprise as my father solemnly handed me the back page of *The Evening Standard*, jabbing a finger at the Test scorecard from Madras. The first four entries read as follows: Fowler, 201; Robinson, 74; Gatting, 207; Lamb, 62. My jaw dropped open and tongue lolled forward. Either they were bloody awful, or we were inspired – whichever, it remains the most glorious English batting card I am ever likely to see.

Completing the triumvirate was Chris Smith, another moustache wearer (although, in fairness, his drooping effort was more in the style of an SAS-trained mercenary touring with the Village People). Having topped the batting averages in the New Zealand leg of England's 1983/84 winter tour, Smith looked set for an extended stay in the side until he lapsed into mediocrity for the subsequent three-Test series against Pakistan. This display of inconsistency, coupled with modest domestic form during the early part of the summer of 1984, eased him out of the running for the Test series. Picked too early, discarded too soon, Chris understood the vagaries of the selectorial merry-go-round that spun throughout English cricket during the 1980s – more slings and arrows than swing and roundabouts – and was determined that his younger brother would not suffer a similar fate. By the time that Chris had played his eighth and final Test, Robin was an established member of the Hampshire side, edging his own way on to the selectorial radar. His match-winning performances in the Benson & Hedges Cup two years later would finally force the issue, earning him an invitation to join a Test side in some disarray.

Gatting had just been sacked over 'barmaidgate' and England were 2-0 down in the series and listing at 80-4 as Smith strode out at Headingley for his debut innings, to face the chin music being drummed up by Marshall, Benjamin, Ambrose and Walsh. He certainly looked the part – the bulky frame, moustache and mullet gave him the reassuringly famil- iar look of an English Test player – but there was something different in his approach to the wicket. The whirling arms and practice shots were nothing new but the neck rotations, the jaw stretches, the gaping eyes, the dancing feet and knee plunges – what was all this? In a word, preparation. Smith's bizarre routine, meticulously planned to ready his mind and body for the unpleasant business of standing up to the leath- ery bombardment that was sure to come, looked incongruous but was clearly effective. Everything was done to excess, he was nimble as a boxer despite his size, his extravagance in evading the danger ball – swaying, bobbing, ducking, dart- ing – was at times balletic and when it was there to be hit, he flayed it to within an inch. At a time when English bats- men too often seemed pinned onto the back foot, the sight of Smith lunging forward to give an errant delivery the full beans was a sight to warm the heart. He could hook and pull well enough, but it was on the off-side where he truly excelled; at times it was butchery. If a bowler dropped one short into the favoured area he would sink to one knee – a genuflection before the sacrifice – before thrashing the ball to the fence with astonishing savagery. From the safety of the stands or sofa, with Smith at the crease, suddenly the West Indian bowlers – the bane and scourge of English batsmen for over a decade – looked, if not quite puppies, then at least mortal.

Described by *Wisden* as a 'season to forget' – the numbers against the West Indies were pretty grim, four different captains, a 4-0 defeat – for two young men at least, thousands of miles from home, striving to make an impression, the summer of 1988 would live long in the memory. Smith's first Tests promised to bring solidity to a middle order starting to creak with age, but an innings in May went further, identifying the man to lead English cricket to the promised land. When the Zimbabwean Graeme Hick confirmed his growing reputation on the county circuit as a rapacious run machine by racking up an unbeaten quadruple century against Somerset at Taunton, the mighty weight of expectation – a burden under which he would stagger for more than a decade – was set. The complexities of the qualification system meant that Hick would not be available to rescue English cricket until the West Indians returned in the summer of 1991. In the meantime the England batting line-up entered an extended period of experimentation. This uncertainty was exacerbated by the continuing controversy over the ties between English cricketers and South Africa. The tour that winter to India was cancelled when Gooch and seven other members of the party were denied visas on account of their previous connections with the Republic. The following summer during the fourth Test of the Ashes series, the band of rebels to be led to South Africa by Mike Gatting was announced.

Ironically the news brought some certainty. The revolving door policy that had blighted the forgettable summer of 1988 – an unlucky thirteen batsmen were tried in various positions in the top six – now had less oil to keep in spinning. The selectors would need to cast their gaze beyond the clutch of batsmen they hauled out of county cricket whenever a stalwart from the Gooch, Gower, Gatting, Lamb stock was unavailable. In short it was time to look forwards, not back. Michael Atherton – the man who would come to symbolise English cricket during the 1990s – was pitched straight into the fray in the fifth Test, arriving with a coffin full of kit marked FEC ('Future England Captain'). Nasser Hussain and Alec Stewart followed soon after, during the winter of redemption in the Caribbean. Ostensibly picked for his batting, the wicket-keeping gauntlets lurking in the latter's kit bag would present the selectors with a puzzle they would never quite solve. The procession of new boys continued with Hick and Mark Ramprakash in 1991 and Graham Thorpe arriving with an impressive century on debut in 1993. Until the top-order class of the 1990s had assembled, Smith bridged the gap between the old and the new – he even clipped the straggling tresses of his mullet – and rapidly came to represent a reassuringly solid presence at the heart of the batting order to match and complement the dependable Gooch at its summit. The mixed fortunes of the team notwithstanding, by 1992 the ICC ratings reckoned them the top two batsmen in Test cricket.

Their talents were tested to the full during the Ashes series of 1989. Blessed with a rare winter of leisure, courtesy of the cancelled tour to India, Gooch had tried his hand at skiing; for Smith the winter sport of choice was sledging. The ruthless streak that Allan Border had instilled in his tourists did not apply simply to the use of bat and ball. Vocal chords were also deployed as a weapon of choice. The value of some well-directed verbals was now recognised as a key part of the psychological warfare needed to thrive in modern Test cricket, and few showed more appetite for the spoken word than fast bowler Mervyn Gregory Hughes. Having been on the receiving end early in his career – Botham swiped him for twenty-two in a single over at the Gabba during the 1986/87 series – Hughes was never happier than when he was getting stuck into the English batsmen. For Merv, the sight of a navy blue batting helmet bearing three lions was like Pavlov clanging a bell. He would slaver under his shaggy, boomerang-shaped moustache, hungry to get at them either with a short-pitched ball rearing at the throat, or a well-chosen rejoinder: 'I'll bowl you a fucking piano, ya Pommie pooftah, let's see if you can play that.' It was during the Lord's Test in 1989 that he finally copped some back. Having recently passed the edge of Smith's bat Merv offered a characteristically forthright critique: 'You can't fucking bat to save your life.' When the next ball sat up and begged, Smith gave generously, leaning into one of his trademark square cuts he thumped it to boundary before calling cheerfully back up the pitch: 'Hey Merv, we make a fine pair. I can't fucking bat and you can't fucking bowl.'

A disaster for the team, the series that begat modern Ashes history was an unequivocal triumph for Smith on a personal level. The verbal jousting with Hughes spurred him on to within four of a century. In his next innings he made up for the disappointment of missing out on a debut century at Lord's by smashing 143 at Old Trafford. The hot streak continued with another ton in the Trent Bridge Test and he would finish the series not out on 77, unbeaten and certainly unbowed. The following summer he added another two centuries against the Indians during a series dominated by the bat, notably the one owned by the England captain. It was in 1990 that Graham Gooch reached his zenith. Entering his third decade as a Test batsman he did not, at first glance, look like a world beater with his bushy moustache, hint of a paunch and slightly florid complexion. A Victorian village bobby admonishing scallywags for scrumping apples with a clip round the ear was nearer the mark – but the numbers tell no lies. His Indian summer was worth an astonishing 752 runs from only three matches, the jewel in this crown his epic 333 at Lord's. But as the next engagement for English cricket was in Australia, it was inevitable that both he and Smith would suffer the lows to follow their highs.

Gooch led a miserable tour characterised by wallopings on the pitch and discord off it, as tensions between himself and David Gower grew. As for Smith, insufficient warm-up games under his belt before the first Test affected his preparation; he lost his touch and then, crucially, his confidence. The player that had thrashed the same bowlers for over 550 runs in the previous Ashes series and held his own in the sledging stakes was now feeling the pressure. A man who clearly appreciated a supporting network of family, friends and mentors, Smith was rarely at his dominant best when playing away from home. A casual glance at his Test career averages – a whisker below fifty in England, mid-thirties elsewhere – tells its own story. Comparisons may be drawn with Marcus Trescothick, an England player of more recent vintage. Off the field both appear genial, untroubled types, on it uncomplicated technicians that, at times, break free to swing the plank with murderous intent. But for whatever reason both men proved susceptible to the whisperings of an inner voice that would often raise its tone to a shout in far flung places.

Ironically it was Smith's emergence from his trough – a century in the match against Queensland capped a nasty run of low scores – that led Gower to don the flying helmet, buzz the ground by way of celebration and plunge the camp back into turmoil.

The following summer against the West Indies, Gooch and Smith began their ascent to the summit of the world order. The series would represent a turning point both in terms of the modern history of the Anglo-Caribbean contest, but perhaps more significantly in the overall status and standing of the West Indian game. A drawn series may not sound like a glorious triumph but England had finally wriggled free of the stranglehold that had squeezed the life out of them since 1976. The bouts that followed during the 1990s would be far more evenly matched until finally, during the Millennial summer, Nasser Hussain stood on the balcony at The Oval holding aloft the Wisden Trophy. The results that have followed this watershed – 10-0 in twelve Tests at the time of writing – speak of England's resurgence under Michael Vaughan, but also of the dramatic and rather sad demise of West Indian cricket.

The century scored by Gooch at Headingley in the first Test of the summer of 1991, carrying his bat to set up an unlikely victory, is widely regarded as one of the finest by an English batman in the modern era. Smith's unbeaten 148 at Lord's in the following match further reinforced the change in the established order. If these efforts had, at least in relative terms, tamed the beast of West Indian fast bowling, the respite would be brief. Like Heracles scything away at the Hydra, the English batsmen would soon enough see fresh dangers rearing up at them.

Devastating though it was, the West Indian line of attack was at least predictable – lightning fast and often pitched nastily short – if not exactly appealing. You could hardly blame them. Nature had blessed the islands with a generation of brilliant practitioners of pace at a time when they were still smarting from a harsh lesson in the vicissitudes of spin bowling. It came in April 1976 at Trinidad where, having watched the Indian spinners operate to good effect on a wearing pitch, the West Indian captain Clive Lloyd unleashed his own trio of twirlers to sew up a routine victory. He then looked on with mounting horror and frustration as his firm of Jumadeen, Padmore and Ali produced 105 overs at a cost of 220 runs, while centurions Gavaskar and Viswanath guided the away side to a winning score of 406 – at the time, the highest total chased for victory. Although the West Indian quick bowlers had been equally culpable in that fourth innings, the scapegoat spinners Ali and Jumadeen were put out to pasture before the deciding final Test in Jamaica. Their replacements – to stretch the livestock metaphor to breaking point – were the snorting bulls Daniel and Holder. The result? Carnage on a grand scale. The simple fact that all seventeen of the Indian touring party were called into service at some point during the game tells its own story. As does the match scorecard, registering the last five Indian batsmen as 'absent hurt'.

As the dominant force in world cricket during the 1970s and 1980s, it was fast bowling (and some bona fide geniuses amongst the batters) that pushed the West Indies to the summit. When Australia took up the mantle in the early 1990s, pace bowling and expertise with the willow was again vital but it was the art of spin that was suddenly, unexpectedly, back in vogue.

'I'd rather be a prick and win,' was the mantra allegedly adopted by Allan Border following the back-to-back Ashes defeats suffered by Australia during the mid-1980s. The uncompromising, workmanlike approach that saw them reclaim the urn in 1989 and retain it in 1991 was still very much in evidence within the party that arrived in 1993. The artisans, however, were now rubbing shoulders with some artists. England fans may not have derived much pleasure from watching their bowlers ground down by the likes of Border and Steve Waugh, but few would argue that the attacking verve of Michael Slater or the classical style of Steve's brother Mark made for unattractive cricket. But it was a bowler, arriving with little experience and less reputation that would, over the next decade and a half, splash brilliant colour across the canvas of world cricket and plunge batsmen, many of them English, into confusion and despair. At first glance the danger was unapparent, as a rather portly figure with a mid-1980s hairdo trotted up to the wicket at Old Trafford and hurled his first Ashes delivery, from the back of his hand, into the air. But when it landed, everything changed. The image of the immediate aftermath of the 'Ball of the Century' is more eloquent than any words. Amidst wild Australian celebration Mike Gatting looks down with a furrowed brow, his lips puckered into an 'o' of disbelief; this is cricket portrayed by Edvard Munch. Having just received the ball that redefined the cliché 'unplayable', Gatting could have been forgiven for pursing his mouth into a 'w' – 'why me?' The 1993 series was his first back in England following the fiascos and farragoes of the previous decade – bickering with umpires, barmaids in hotels, rebel tours – and now he had inadvertently wandered in front of the greatest delivery in the history of cricket. One wonders what (if anything) the dazed and confused Gatting murmured, *en passant*, to Robin Smith, as he trudged back to the pavilion. Some practical advice? 'Watch the chunky lad, he gives it a bit of a tweak'; Introspection?, 'the horror, the horror'; Prescience? '*après moi, le deluge*'. In any event, Smith would soon be taking the long walk himself. Caught at slip after prodding forward to another Warne special, his walk back to the dressing room would be tinged with a sense of déjà vu. Smith knew that his demise was not attributable simply to a freakish wonderball but to a deeper malaise that would drag him gradually down from the heights – as he made that walk he was still ranked the fifth-best batsman in world cricket with an average of just under fifty – and cast a shadow across the remainder of his Test career.

During the previous summer against the Pakistanis, all of the English batsmen had struggled to come to terms with the high-speed swing generated by Wasim and Waqar but it was Mushtaq Ahmed – another barrel-shaped bundle of trouble – that had given Smith particular problems. Smith's cricketing upbringing, subsequent experience and motivational techniques had equipped him with the courage and skills to succeed at a time when speed was still the most valuable currency in Test-match bowling. But one-by-one a generation of geniuses arrived at the crease – Kumble, Warne, Mushtaq, Murali – with fingers twisting and wrists contorting, their sleight of hand producing ever more lavish deceptions; at times they had the ball on a string and the batsmen in their pocket, both dancing to their mesmerising tune. As ever, the numbers take no prisoners: an average of 52 for the first four years of Smith's international career slumps to 37 for the remaining five, as the twists and turns of this new menace took their toll.

For a man often beset by worries over loss of form and his place in the side, Smith's uncertainties in front of the spinners gnawed away at his confidence. This sense of transience can only have been heightened by his travels up and down the batting order during the later years of his Test career.

Settled and successful at no.4, he suffered more than most as the selectors endlessly shuffled their pack trying to play the ace promised by Alec Stewart's skills with bat and keeping gloves. This unsettling role as a utility player – in his last nine matches he appeared in every slot in the top six – saw Smith's contribution recede from the spectacular to the merely solid. Even his last great hurrah, a monumental 175 in Antigua during the 1993/94 tour, was overshadowed, being exactly 200 runs short of Brian Lara's world record in the first innings.

When Smith entered the dangerous world inhabited by the English Test side at the end of the 1980s he found it well suited to his carefully honed skills. The physical assaults of Curtly and Courtney, Wasim and Waqar, and verbal volleys from Border's ruthless outfit were met head on, without a flinch. During the 1990s in cricket, as in politics, spin would emerge as a potent force. Built for tree-felling rather than trifling with the intricacies of googlies, flippers, doosras and chinamen, Smith struggled to cope with the emergent menace. A game he had constructed with great care upon the solid foundations of certainty and confidence – purposeful movements back and forward, asserting ownership of the crease – lacked the nimble feet and wristy finesse needed to manage the subtle deceptions of a skilfully spun ball. These difficulties notwithstanding, he maintained an impressive personal record during a difficult period for English cricket and, together with his brother, was a stalwart of the Hampshire side. When in July 1991 the ICC announced that South Africa were to be re-admitted into international cricket, their rankings algorithm rated Smith as the second-best batsman in the world; there can be little doubt that the South Africa's loss was undoubtedly England's gain.

TEN

ACCIDENTAL HERO

Of the many legends associated with the late George Best, the one most likely to endure as his epitaph goes something like this: a young bellboy enters the plush suite of a casino hotel to find a room strewn with empty champagne bottles, lingerie and cash; in the bed Best is slumbering next to the current Miss World. Opening a bleary eye, the Manchester United legend espies the third party in the room. The young man is eying him with reproach, 'George, where did it all go wrong?' I can't help but wonder if, when the Zimbabwean-born batsman Graeme Hick departs a cricket field for the final time – carrying over 40,000 first-class runs, a century of centuries and countless other records with him – a similar question will await him at the boundary's edge. Whichever way you look at Hick's career, difficult questions remain unanswered.

In the early days life was straightforward enough. Hick became an established, then indispensable, member of the

Worcestershire side and the whispering campaign around the county circuit started to gather pace. By the late 1980s it had risen to a clamour, the Zimbabwean prodigy must qualify for England; with him in the side we would be unstoppable. Of course the shy, unassuming young man was not clambering aboard this pedestal, or revelling in his messianic status. Indeed, the opposite is nearer the truth. As judgment day approached in 1991 a dip in his form forewarned of the damaging effects of the great expectations he carried but he just could not help scoring runs. Lots of them. As early as 1985, during a summer of split duties between Worcestershire and the touring Zimbabweans, his 230 against Oxford University at the Parks in the colours of his country revealed a hunger for runs that he is still trying to satisfy over twenty years later.

The following season he became the youngest player to score 2,000 first-class runs in a season, moving *Wisden* to name him as one of their cricketers of the year; in 1987 he proved his mettle in the shortened game, averaging almost sixty as Worcestershire topped the Sunday League. They retained this title the following summer and, more significantly, collected their first County Championship since their coach Basil D'Oliveira had celebrated this feat as a player in 1974. It was during this year that Hick confirmed the breadth of his talent in spectacular and extreme fashion. A blitz against Surrey at The Oval earned him the Walter Lawrence Trophy for the season's fastest century but it was at Taunton in late spring that he effectively sealed his fate as the heir apparent to the superhero cape last seen draped over Botham's brawny shoulders in 1981. Hick's monstrous innings of 405 not out at Taunton in the first week of May landed with a reassuring thud in the collective psyche of the English cricket fan – soon enough everything would be alright, we had found ourselves a Bradman.

Any doubts as to Hick's superhuman status that lingered after the quadruple century – perhaps he had simply caught a modest county attack on an off day? – were soon swept away in the weeks that followed. Needing only 180-odd runs to complete the celebrated 1,000 runs in May, an unexpected sequence of failures suddenly presented him with the daunting task of finding more than 150 in the last match of the month. To add spice, the visitors to New Road were the West Indies, warming up against the counties ahead of another summer of sport with the English Test batsmen. At the close of play on the first day Hick stood unbeaten on 172. Now it was official. Here was a man that could even tame the Caribbean tempest – Walsh, Ambrose, Patterson and Bishop all toiled in vain that day – and would, no doubt, make equally short work of anything else that international cricket dared to throw at him. He was an artist, an alchemist, a contender, above all, he was an Englishman, or would be by 1991.

Hick made good use of his remaining summers of qualification in the blissful purgatory of county cricket. In 1989 his
contribution of 1,500 runs helped Worcestershire retain their
Championship title; the following year over 2,000 runs at an
average of 90 further whet the appetite for his forthcoming
bow on the international stage. At the time, the only man
that could match his consistent and gluttonous scoring was
Jimmy Cook, a South African quietly rewriting the record
books at Somerset.

If this description of the expectation levels that rose like
flood waters ahead of Hick's Test debut sounds over the top,
it's probably because they were. Gross exaggeration is, of
course, a vital element in the reporting of professional sport.
Back pages rarely carry headlines like 'Nice, solid performance earns goalless draw' – the media delivers what we, as
fans, demand: heroes and villains, winners and losers, idols
and scapegoats. Players must take their place, if only briefly, in
one or other of these extreme categories. Look at the career
of David Beckham, the most iconic British sportsman this
century has produced so far. At first the darling of the tabloids – scoring from the halfway line, with a Spice Girl on
his arm – they piked him as the 'stupid boy' whose red card
dashed our chances at the 1998 World Cup, but welcomed
back 'Goldenballs' after his free kick had curled us into the
next. Fair play, at the end of the day, as Becks himself might
say. Looking on helplessly from the sidelines, as fans we invest

vast amounts of hope and cash in our sporting idols – we have paid for the privilege of pointing out their failings. As penalties are ballooned over crossbars, catches dropped and 3ft putts missed, we sink from the sofa to our knees, face cradled in hands cursing their ineptitude, and we do so as of right.

Hick was, almost certainly, hyped beyond the boundaries of realism ahead of his England debut. The 'Great White Hope' tag had been slapped on his back long before he walked out to face the West Indies at Headingley, early in the summer of 1991. The final chapter of an autobiography (published in 1991, no doubt to mark his elevation onto the main stage) carries the loaded title, *England Expects*. While a characteristically straight bat is evident within the prose, between the lines one can also detect the unwritten pleas – 'Give me a chance, don't judge too soon, I can't promise miracles overnight' – of a man desperate to prove wrong the negative whisperings acting as the counterpoint to the groundswell of expectation.

The Headingley Test was full of positives for England – Gooch's seminal century, eight wickets for DeFreitas and a home victory, finally, over the West Indies – but disappointing on a personal level for Hick. A dozen runs spread evenly across two innings was hardly the stuff of dreams. Nightmarish would better describe a duck at Lord's in the following Test. Desperate to find a foothold in the international game he dug in at Trent Bridge and grafted away for almost three hours to reach 43, a healthy confidence builder, wrecked by another globe in the second innings. Two more failures at Edgbaston pushed him into unchartered territory – the run machine was grinding along at an average of 10. By contrast, what followed would, over the coming years, become painfully familiar. He was dropped.

The selectorial hokey-cokey that blighted, and possibly doomed, the Test careers of Hick and Mark Ramprakash (another prodigy blooded that summer) was a constant thread running through the blanket of gloom that hung over English cricket for much of the 1990s. The paradox that trapped them ran something like this: dropped from the international squad, their brilliance in county cricket saw them recalled to the Test side; moderate form returned them to the shires, where their prolific scoring would soon demand a recall to the… and so on. Like most armchair Olympians, I assume the answers to such sporting quandaries must be easy to come by. Remote control in one hand, the other bunched into an angry little fist shaking at the television, I know what's best. Of course I do. But certain facts are beyond doubt, Hick and Ramprakash carried with them the two golden talents of their generation, both required careful handling to encourage these gifts to flourish and they finished with Test averages of 31 and 27 respectively. Something went wrong there. In Hick's case things started to drift when he got the boot after only seven innings.

A man as familiar with the talent and temperament of the young Hick as he was with the concept of playing cricket for England as an 'outsider' under the burden of immense and peculiar pressures, Basil D'Oliveira, then coach at Worcestershire, recognised the need for some patience: 'All Graeme needs is an early hundred for England and then we can all settle down and watch him become one of the greats.' Those a little closer to the England camp did not need to look too hard for relevant precedents supporting this perseverance principle. When England won the Ashes in 1986/87 three half centuries from a twenty-one-year-old in the home side's middle order suggested to the Australian selectors that he might have something they could use. They stuck with him, despite the fact that, by the time the rematch with England came around in 1989 he had failed, in 26 matches, to produce a Test century. And then the dam broke. His commanding, unbeaten centuries in the first two matches of the series did much to establish a period of Australian supremacy that would run until 2005. By the time he was finished with England, and Test cricket, his 10,927 runs made Steve Waugh the most prolific batsman in the history of the game.

For Hick the first of many recalls arrived immediately. England's winter tour of New Zealand and Australia brought mixed blessings. In the Test series against the Kiwis he made a number of good starts with the bat, then failed to convert them into the kind of contribution that can turn a match, but his worth as a second spinner was proved. As the party moved on to Australia for the World Cup, his three half centuries were critical in propelling England to the final. The tour, in short, encapsulated the frustrations felt by observers of Hick's nascent international career – some useful wickets and decent one-day form but where was the promised avalanche of Test runs? Of course Hick himself had made no promises; that early autobiography begs for patience ahead of any judgement, reckoning that a couple of years would produce a meaningful yardstick by which to measure his development. An average of ten against the West Indies had risen to about thirty against New Zealand – progress was being made, if not history – and the improvement continued in his second home series when he hit a maiden half century against Pakistan. In a series dominated by the lavishly dangerous swing generated by Wasim and Waqar, all of the English batsmen struggled but it was Hick, for the second summer running, that was handed the pink slip before the series had run its course.

A few months later he was on a plane bound for India, recalled to the fold thanks in no small part to the need for spinning options on the dustbowl wickets of the subcontinent. The selectorial side bet came good as he topped the averages with bat and ball. Most significantly, his 178 in the third Test at Bombay would surely prove the catalyst for the success that Basil D'Oliveira had predicted. But in common with too many of the key moments in Hick's Test career, the moment had soon passed; the point at which all would step back and say, 'yes, he's arrived' remained elusive. We're back to the numbers game which dictates that, in cricket, one hundred is an unequal sum. Gooch's century against the West Indies in 1991 and Atherton's against South Africa during the 1995/96 tour were, in the most literal sense, remarkable: they ticked all the major boxes – courage, skill, composure, determination – but most of all they directed the course of the match. Unquestionably a magnificent piece of batsmanship, Hick's first and largest Test century came in a match that England would lose handsomely to complete a 3-0 drubbing on a tour they simply could not wait to forget. The curse of the forgotten century would strike again in November 1995 as Hick, to coin the term used by Allan Donald, 'hammered' the South African bowling attack all over Centurion Park for a next-best Test knock of 141. I well remember the delight creasing Hicks' countenance – too often clouded with apprehension and frustration – as he was interviewed on television at the close of the day's play, a centurion on his return to Africa as a Test player, nothing could spoil the moment. Then rain of Biblical proportions swept in, the match and its highlight were washed away. By contrast the twenty-nine runs scored by Jack Russell in support of Mike Atherton's career-defining rearguard innings at Johannesburg in the following Test is imprinted on the subconscious of many more England fans than Hick's century at Centurion Park ever will be.

The Ashes summer of 1993 would heap more misery upon English cricket. The Australian top six – Taylor, Slater, Boon, Border the Waugh twins – filled their boots time and again, Warne conjured confusion and uncertainty, Merv Hughes barked away in the field, seeking chinks in the mental armoury of the English batsmen. By now the Australians were refining the weaponry they dragged into the fray. The dangers that bat and ball offered to inflict were, to an extent, ameliorated by the availability of protective equipment; with the possible exception of a good shrink, there was little to safeguard a player against a sustained assault on his psyche. Recognising the adage of a game played as much in the mind as on the pitch, 'mental disintegration' – a term, and concept, thought to have had its origins during Border's take-no-prisoners tour of 1989, but most strongly associated with Steve Waugh's captaincy – was the desired result. The Australians had clearly seen enough of Hick to glimpse cracks that could be probed. Merv Hughes led the charge in the First Test at Old Trafford, sustaining a verbal attack – he would later admit to having been 'a bit OTT with Hick' – of such intensity that umpire Dickie Bird was moved to enquire what 'that nice Mr Hick' had ever done to him. One of the defining images of the summer depicts Hick, shoulders slumped, trudging from the crease. Millimetres behind him Hughes is in pursuit bellowing a tirade of sweet somethings down the back of his neck. Despite the bespoke pressures the Australians added to those he was always destined to operate under, Hick's return from the first two Tests – 34, 22, 20 and 64 – was solid enough. But with the Ashes slipping from their grasp yet again, the selectors took a long hard look at the English dressing room, grabbed the new broom and proceeded to swing it with wild abandon. At Trent Bridge debuts were handed to Ilott, Lathwell, McCague and Thorpe, while Nasser Hussain was recalled having been discarded as a failed prodigy three years earlier. Licking their wounds on the other side of the revolving door sat Mike Gatting, probably still groggy from the shock of Warne's über ball, and Hick.

If any selection defines the quick-fix policy that too often prevailed in extremis for England at this time it is that of Mark Lathwell during the summer of 1993. The twenty-one-year-old had shown great promise during the 'A' Tour the previous winter and was an emerging talent in the Somerset team; quite how this qualified him to open the batting in a must-win Test match for a side pinned to the wall by opponents superior on all counts is a mystery. In fairness, England did manage to draw the match, thanks to centuries from Gooch and Thorpe, the latter displaying a bloody-minded determination that England would cherish during the decade that followed. To his credit Lathwell made useful, if not decisive, contributions in each innings, but when England were tonked in the next Test at Leeds, the Ashes were bound for Australia and the young man was heading back to Somerset and obscurity.

The scattergun selection policy then fired Matthew Maynard (not seen since a Test debut in 1988) and the forty-something John Emburey into the mix for a defeat at Edgbaston, before launching Hick back into proceedings for the final match at The Oval. England's victory provided some crumbs of comfort but, for Hick, a hundred runs in the match – to secure a series average of over forty – can only have left a rather sour taste at his hasty ejection from proceedings halfway though the summer. Perhaps recognising the shortcomings of their knee-jerk approach the selectors now granted him an extended, unbroken, run in the team. His form was sound during the winter tour of the Caribbean, but it was during England's historic meeting with the 'new' South Africa the following summer that he really rose to the occasion. A century at Headingley helped set up a sporting declaration, but the match would end in a draw. Crucially he followed this with an unbeaten 81 off as many balls as England chased a target to secure victory in the third and final Test to square the series. Even then fate poked a bony finger into the Hick ribcage – the post-match adulation and credit was all channelled in one direction. Devon Malcolm, roused into a lethal assault on the South Africans following a smack on the kettle whilst batting, had run in like a man possessed, grabbing nine wickets and all the headlines in the process.

For the first time since his trumpeted arrival in the England camp Hick was starting to look and feel like he belonged there. In many ways this fulfilled his own prophecy. He had reckoned ahead of his debut that he would need two years to establish himself; thanks to the vacillations of the selectors those two years had taken three years to complete. Confidence in his form and comfort in his place in the side would provide valuable resources from which to draw during the toughest possible series to follow, an Ashes battle Down Under. The size of the task became immediately evident at Brisbane in the first Test. Australia were in control from the first ball – Michael Slater slapped a loosener from Phil DeFreitas gleefully to the fence – to the last, with Shane Warne trapping Darren Gough leg-before to collect an eleventh wicket in the match. The second Test went the same way as England were despatched for 92 on the final day, making the Sydney Test an engagement in the last-chance saloon. After a decent first knock from the visitors, suddenly it was Australia leaning back on the ropes as Gough collected six wickets, a dashing fifty, and damnation in the shape of a 'next Botham' tag. This was rather exotic Ashes territory, England on top looking to press home their advantage. They did so as Atherton and Hick put on 150 for the second wicket, the latter picking up on the good touch he had shown in Brisbane, where he had laboured for ten minutes shy of five hours against Warne's twirling torments. England's no.3 was starting to bat with the kind of authority that had brought bowlers on the English county circuit to their knees over the previous decade. But even then, standing at the wicket seemingly inured to the thousand natural shocks presented by Test cricket – rearing bouncers, demonic spin, personalised sledging, expectant crowds, fickle selectors – he was caught by a beauty, right in the breadbasket. Wallop! Atherton had departed the scene and was pacing the dressing room, growing anxious that England were not progressing with sufficient purpose towards an unassailable position from which to declare. Hick had been making steady, if not sprightly, progress towards a cathartic, first Ashes century, and on 98 – having faced precisely the same number of deliveries as Atherton had in compiling his 67 – stood on the brink. At which point the captain called them in.

It might have helped Graeme Hick, during the darker and less explicable moments in his Test career to have had Heller's sage observation from *Catch 22* inscribed, for ease of reference, on the palm of one of his batting gloves: 'The enemy is anybody who's going to get you killed, no matter which side he's on.' If Hick had already harboured suspicions concerning the level of support he enjoyed within the England camp, Atherton's declaration must have nudged him in the direction of conspiracy theories. The decision even left Alec Stewart bemused, his autobiography describes the move as 'the worst thing that could have happened to both the player and team.' On returning to the field the tourists could not find the spark to pressurise the Australians and the openers soon rattled up 200 to scupper English hopes of victory. As for Hick, injury forced him to watch the remaining matches of the series from the sidelines – yet another incomplete series – brooding, wondering, questioning.

Back in England the following summer, during an evenly matched contest with a West Indian side easing inexorably into a long and slow decline, the testy relationship between the English establishment and Hick continued. Following a heavy defeat at Edgbaston he reacted to the familiar news that he was to be dropped by departing the dressing room with tears in his eyes. He was further stung by the team manager Ray Illingworth's assertion that this reaction proved Hick had a 'soft centre'. Hick requested a meeting with Illingworth two days before the following match to make his case for a recall; the answer, in brief, was 'prove me wrong'. The unbeaten century that followed suggested to the coaching staff that they had struck gold – it was the stick that Hick needed, not the carrot – but they had not. Following the conclusion of his Test career when Hick was asked in a BBC interview to name the best Test match coaches he had player under, he replied: 'That's the trouble, there haven't been any.' A firm, guiding hand deployed with empathy and encouragement was needed; in his dealings with the young Hick it seems only Basil D'Oliveira found the necessary formula.

In spite of everything, as the year drew to a close, Hick was nosing around the pantheon housing Test cricket's leading batsmen; in the ICC Test ratings he sat seventh and third within the one-day fraternity. As 1996 dawned it seemed that he was finally ready to haul another cliché out of the sporting closet and 'take his game to the next level'. He began well in May, thrashing a double century in Worcestershire's fixture against England's next opponents. Arguably one of the least threatening propositions in world cricket, the Indians bowling on green, English wickets promised to provide him with many more runs when the Test series began. At which point, in a typically perverse twist, his form utterly collapsed. Following a lean run – 8, 1, 6, 20, 4 and 4 in six innings against India and Pakistan was positively emaciated – the selectors had seen enough. Harshly jettisoned in previous years, this time the brick they dropped was at least tepid and would now be left to cool for a year and a half. The timing of his exclusion could not have been worse. That winter England made an historic tour to Zimbabwe; for Hick there would be no glorious homecoming.

The following summer normal service resumed on all fronts. Hick scored over 1,500 first-class runs at just under seventy, the highlight a triple century against Hampshire and the selectors came calling. They had now refined their view of the man who, it had been hoped, would be the lynchpin of the Test batting order, preferring to see him as a one-day specialist. As such, he was a key figure in the side that Adam Hollioake led to victory in the Champions Trophy in

Sharjah. Comfortable in this new role, during the late summer of 1998 he was, rather unexpectedly, crowbarred back into the Test side for the final two tests of a scintillating series with South Africa. An important contest in the context of the jostling for position in the pack chasing the Australians, the series also served as a warm-up for that winter's Ashes. Nine runs in three knocks suggested that Hick had lost his final chance to prove himself in the heat of battle, but a century in a one-off match against Sri Lanka gave the selectors a familiar headache.

They opted for Lancashire's John Crawley – a prolific county player with undoubted talent, his flattery to deceive at Test level made him Hick's natural successor – but would be forced to call upon the Worcestershire man as cover when Atherton's perennial back problem flared. Unlike many that had gone before, the 1998/99 Ashes series did at least smoulder for all five Tests. With the opener at Brisbane drawn in the rain, Australian victories at Perth and Adelaide prefaced a famous England victory at Melbourne. Although Hick's 60 in the second innings was crucial in providing Australia with a target worth chasing, the dynamic burst from Dean Headley that shattered their middle order inevitably claimed the lion's share of the plaudits.

Later that year the man from Zimbabwe would take a firm grip on the England team ushering in a period of unprecedented success that would reach its pinnacle with a cathartic reclamation of the Ashes. The man in question was not Hick but Duncan Fletcher, the coach eased into the hot seat vacated by David Lloyd, following England's turgid performance at a World Cup in which much had been expected of the host nation.

By the Millennial summer the green shoots of recovery were evident. Victory against a thoroughly demoralised Zimbabwean side proved little, but it was during the main event – five Tests against the West Indies – that Fletcher's players visibly grew in confidence and stature. The summer would also signal the start of the final chapter in the deeply unsatisfactory story of Graeme Hick's international career. It began positively with a century at Lord's but, ironically, murdering an inferior Zimbabwean bowling attack in friendly conditions was simply further grist to the mill for his detractors. Early in his career, Hick's perceived penchant for pulverising the weak had led the former New Zealand Test player John Bracewell to hang an albatross around the young man's neck, to clunk loudly against that already swinging there marked, 'Great White Hope'. The 'flat-track bully' tag would provide the leitmotif to the chorus of discontented groans that dogged Hick's attempts to satisfy the lavish expectations he had unwittingly dragged into the Test arena. When the serious business began that summer at Edgbaston, the West Indies, inspired by hostile bowling from the old warhorse Courtney Walsh, galloped to victory and Hick's pair seemed to uphold this charge of selective greatness. In a series dominated by breathtaking bowling displays, his one contribution of note – a steady 59 at Headingley batting down at eight, sharing a key partnership with Michael Vaughan – was soon forgotten in the aftermath of Andy Caddick's insane spell of 4-15 that fired England to victory and the lead in the series.

Almost a decade after he had stepped blinking into the glare of Test match cricket at an expectant Headingley, it was the gathered gloom of Karachi that saw Graeme Hick play his last significant innings for England. The enduring image of the match – a victory for England to secure an improbable series win – was of a grinning Graham Thorpe, dragging his exhausted carcass from the field in virtual darkness accompanied by his jubilant skipper Nasser Hussain. Elsewhere in the shadows Hick could enjoy the satisfaction of reliving a long vigil spent with Thorpe, eking out forty crucial runs, before falling to Waqar as the game edged into its final act. This was not, of course, the role that many had envsiaged for Worcestershire's run machine when he had qualified to play for England – a doughty support act to grind out a narrow victory. His part was to have been the lead, the virtuoso, the powerhouse of the batting order, driving his team on to emphatic victories and sending shudders through opposing bowling attacks.

The fact that before, during and after his Test career Hick performed precisely this part for his county, fuels the fire that rages around his modest record on the international stage. For many, the answer lies in the extended apprenticeship that he served on the domestic circuit during the long years of qualification. Steve Waugh, for one, whose dogged ascent of Test cricket's learning curve in his early years served him so handsomely, felt that the county game left Hick ill-prepared for the sterner challenges that followed.

Any such discussion of the gaps in Hick's technique will, eventually, settle on his perceived Achilles heel – the short-pitched ball. A lethal weapon in Test cricket – especially during the supremacy of the West Indian quicks – the regulations in the county game offered some degree of protection aganst this menace. For Hick's baptism of fire in Test cricket Messrs Marshall, Patterson, Ambrose and Walsh set to work on a lively top in Leeds, unfettered by the limits on skull-crushing bouncers. Hick's stature at the crease, as a 6ft 3in, broad-shouldered giant had rattled the county attacks; faced with serious pace and nasty, steepling bounce he suddenly looked vunerable, rigidly upright, stuck in the line of fire. In that first series the eyes of fast bowlers around the world narrowed, sensing a weakness – the knight riding to England's rescue had a chink in his shining armour.

Although he has played over 500 first-class games, this brief review of Graeme Hick's impact on English cricket has focussed on his travails in the international game. Why? Well, it's a good story, highs and lows, triumph then disaster, intrigue and confusion. By contrast his adventures in first-class cricket are dreadfully dull – unparalleled success, numerous titles, a succession of broken records. For many, the simplest solution to the puzzle underlying the great Hick debate is to fall back on the Churchillian view of Russia – 'a riddle wrapped in a mystery inside an enigma' – and leave it at that. Simple yes, satisfactory no. A man described as a bully was not, despite his stature and power, an aggressive or overbearing character. Quite the opposite. If he was ever to have made good on the promise so evident when he entered the Test arena, a far more thoughtful and careful approach in nurturing his talent was required by the England management. But it was not to be. As it was, for Graeme Hick, the necessary strands of a successful career at the highest level – talent, temperament, luck – somehow contrived to twist and tighten into a Gordian Knot. It left a feeling of disappointment, regret and far too many loose ends.

ELEVEN

EASE AND GRACE

Strictly speaking, the chivalric rules of engagement suggest that the passing of a glove between protagonists acts as a prelude to hostilities; the throwing down of the gauntlet. In 1998, following a breathtaking duel with Allan Donald, Mike Atherton reversed the convention, sending the pace bowler one of the batting gloves he had worn during their set-to. This was neither a fresh call to arms nor an attempted sleight, rather an acknowledgment of the role played by luck in top-flight sport, most notably in a passage of play that defined the contest between England and South Africa after the latter had returned to the world of Test cricket. The juicy red stain on the glove, encircled, signed by Atherton and presented to Donald as an item for auction during his benefit year, confirmed the fast bowler's suspicions; an umpiring error at a crucial moment had blessed the batsman and damned the bowler.

Over many years the battle between Atherton and Donald epitomised the struggle between their respective countries to emerge as the leading challenger to Australian dominance. The tall, rangy fast bowler from the Free State combined a natural athleticism with a gently simmering aggression. The spearhead of South Africa's drive to reassert themselves in global cricket following the years in isolation, Donald personified the hunger for success felt by the players and the country. Waiting for him twenty-two yards away stood Mike Atherton – resilient, uncomplicated, and stubborn as a mule. Like Boycott before him, Atherton represented a particular breed: the English batsman whose worth is only truly appreciated after he has departed the scene. He was the obdurate rock at the top of the order, hugely reassuring for team-mates, deeply irritating to opponents. The breathtaking scrap between Donald and Atherton at Trent Bridge during the 1998 series – Donald pounding away maddened by a sense of injustice, Atherton pinned in his corner, gloves up, weathering the storm – was simply the highlight of a long, well-matched bout.

It was a storm that had raged over the Midlands for some years as Donald, nicknamed 'Vit Blitz' (White Lightning in Afrikaans), developed into one of the most feared bowlers on the county circuit and helped Warwickshire to become the supreme force in English cricket. A long stay seemed unlikely when the gangling twenty-year-old bowler first arrived in Birmingham in the spring of 1987. Recognised as a prodigy back home, having recently ruffled the feathers of an Australian rebel side, he was a complete unknown in England. What's more, Warwickshire already had a fast bowler from overseas in the side, the Antiguan Tony Merrick. For two seasons Donald struggled to settle into both the team and the culture of English cricket – grassy pitches, post-match beers and even the English language were all novelties to a young man raised in the stultifying heat and rigid conservatism of Bloemfontein. But in the summer of 1989 everything fell into place. His battle with Merrick looked won when the West Indian fell foul of the Warwickshire establishment, arriving late and out of shape for the new season. By contrast Donald had spent the winter at home polishing the weaponry he aimed to unleash on the unsuspecting batsmen of the county circuit. Working with Clive Rice, he developed an outswinger bespoke for English conditions. At Warwickshire, further encouragement was provided by his skipper Andy Lloyd. Having lost consciousness and his Test place on the same morning at Edgbaston earlier in the 1980s (rapped on the skull by that Marshall bouncer) Lloyd nurtured the talented destroyer in his own ranks. Lloyd's repeated mantra 'ease and grace' urged his young firebrand to focus on the rhythm in his approach to the stumps rather than raw pace. The tutelage and careful handling worked. Donald collected 86 wickets in the County Championship at just over sixteen.

In addition, fourteen wickets at less than ten apiece helped Warwickshire to secure the NatWest Trophy – the first of many successes for a county assembling a group of players that would, in time, sweep the board.

That winter it was a different set of players that occupied the attention of the cricket-following world. 'An ill-timed venture' was the verdict of the editorial to that year's *Wisden*, on Mike Gatting's rebel tour to South Africa. Opposed by the ANC, its coincidence with the release of Nelson Mandela only added to the tensions surrounding this momentous event in South African history. Charging in to pepper the rebels, Donald harboured mixed emotions. The thrill of facing up to international opposition was tempered with concerns at the dubious political wisdom of staging such a series at that time.

In the end the tour was curtailed ahead of schedule, but its architect, Dr Ali Bacher, skipper of the golden side of 1970 comprising Richards, Procter et al (in short, a man who knew what talent looked like), recognised the important role that men like Donald would have to play in the future of South African cricket. Knowing that the young fast bowler could see his compatriots on the English county circuit enjoying Test cricket under a foreign flag, Bacher counselled patience, assuring Donald that the day when he would walk out wearing the Protea badge in an official international match was fast approaching.

Sure enough, in July 1991 the ICC announced the readmission of South Africa into the international cricketing fraternity and although they would not return as the 'Boks', the aptly named Proteas represented the flowering of an era of change. The news spurred Donald on to another dazzling summer in the counties, claiming 83 wickets at nineteen as Warwickshire narrowly lost out to Essex in the Championship race. The nucleus of a useful side that had gathered at the turn of the decade had now burgeoned into a multi-talented unit with match-winning skills in all departments.

In Dermot Reeve they had an all-rounder with a competitive edge on which to sharpen blades. An astute tactician with a penchant for winding up opponents, as soon as he had succeeded Andy Lloyd as captain, Reeve employed both qualities to push Warwickshire to the pinnacle of the domestic game. His bloody-minded determination to prevail irrespective of the consequences had revealed itself during a Championship fixture with Northamptonshire early in the summer of 1990. Some word or gesture had enraged the lethally quick Antiguan Curtly Ambrose into hurling a trio of beamers at Reeve's upper body. Having called for a chest pad, the batsman progressed to a double century; the bowler stalked from the field in disgust.

For the Warwickshire team, the summer of 1991 foretold of their dominance in the coming years; for Donald a nomination as one of the *Wisden* cricketers of the year ratified his status as one of the leading talents in the English game.

South Africa's rehabilitation into international competition was boosted by an impressive showing in the 1992 World Cup, beating the hosts Australia in their opening game and eventually losing to England in the semi-final. Even then their demise was somewhat unfortunate as a rain delay, and the application of a mathematical formula designed to account for such meteorological interventions, left them needing twenty-six runs from a single ball. And that, as they say, is a big ask – even for Mike Procter in his late-1970s pomp.

By the summer of 1993, Reeve's mark was clearly evident on the Warwickshire side that hung on to the bitter end to win a classic NatWest Trophy final against Sussex. Their leading strike bowler, however, was absent from the champagne soakings in the dressing room at Lord's. While his teammates were over the moon, Donald was across the globe in Colombo, as the demands of national service called him away from his domestic duties.

In the summer of 1994 Donald's two professional worlds came together as South Africa arrived in England for an historic tour. Led by the granite-hard Kepler Wessels, the Proteas had long since passed the 'glad to be back' stage. Now they were looking for results. At Lord's they found one. Perhaps it was a whiff of the censorious old colonial power, issuing edicts from the final bastion of establishment England. The tourists were banned from draping the 'Rainbow Nation' flag over their dressing room balcony and even Desmond Tutu was delayed briefly, as he strolled through the pavilion to lead the tourists in prayer before play. A man of God he may be, but that was no excuse for sauntering through the Long Room without a jacket or a tie.

The Proteas took control from the first day and never looked back, thanks to a dogged century from their captain – the innings of a man playing out his destiny. Wessels had played at Lord's for Sussex during the late 1970s and returned in the mid-1980 as a member of the Australian team beaten to the Ashes. Now in the twilight of his career, captaining the country of his birth, he spent the best part of five hours meticulously collecting a century of runs to bring his cricketing journey to a satisfactory conclusion. England's response was less inspiring, skittled out for 180 as Donald ran riot, collecting five wickets in fewer than twenty overs. Once South Africa had batted again, the task facing the English batsmen, as they returned to the crease, was simple enough: heads down, survive, tough it out on Sunday afternoon and pray for rain on Monday. And then they were bowled out for 99.

If the capitulation in the second innings at Lord's showed up their frailties, the rousing finale that England produced in the third Test at The Oval demonstrated another quality often evident in British teams, perhaps best described by a recent addition to the dictionary of football manager-speak: bouncebackability. Mike Atherton had already posted a stinging riposte to the flack he had taken over the 'dirt in the pocket' incident (surely only an English sport could spawn a scandal with such an unappetising name) by grinding out a cussed 99 in the drawn second Test at Headingley.

When Athers chalked up his 'flake' at Leeds (if this is not already the designated slang for a score one short of a century, it should be) he completed a hat-trick of sorts and scored a hollow victory in that particular round of cricket's numbers game. The dire score his entire team cobbled together in losing the Lord's Test was the second in a sequence that had begun for Atherton during the Ashes series the previous summer at the same venue. It was here that he stumbled halfway down the wicket looking for the crucial run, slipped, recovered, slipped again and was run out to a chorus of joyous hooting from the Australians. An incident that epitomised England's hapless Ashes experiences during the 1990s it was, at least, beautifully framed by the dulcet, Welsh tones of Tony Lewis in the BBC commentary box: 'Like running in a nightmare; feet caught up in bedclothes'.

Atherton's side had already shown a gift for clambering out the wreckage of humiliating defeat on to the victory rostrum. In March they had been bombed out for 46 (only one better than the all-time nadir from 1887) as Curtly Ambrose went berserk at Port of Spain. Yet in the very next match at Barbados, a brace of centuries from Alec Stewart saw England triumph in Georgetown for the first time and by a healthy margin too. Several months later at The Oval it was another tour de force from a West-Indian-born fast bowler, this time on England's side, that won the match and squared the series. Having received a bouncer that had rattled his teeth and sent him down for a closer inspection of the pitch, Jamaican-born Devon Malcolm emerged from the red mist to bowl a spell so memorable that I doubt he has paid for a drink since. By contrast, Donald limped away from the match with cramp in his calves and a ringing in his ears. The former had restricted his ability to steam in at England as they chased down the manageable target left by Malcolm's furious assault. Wessels interpreted this as weakness at a time of the team's greatest need, and left his strike bowler in no doubt as to his feelings.

The pendulous swing of form and fortune evident in the historic 1994 series characterised the subsequent meetings between England and South Africa. Bullied by the West Indies and Australia during their one-sided affairs of the 1980s and 1990s, the relationship the English side has developed with the Proteas is more complex and meaningful. With the West Indies slipping into mediocrity and the mercurial talents of the Asian nations too often unreliable in foreign climes, the scuffles between England and South Africa seemed to carry a certain weight. They are the pretenders to the title, eyeing Australia patting its stomach at the top table, sparring for the right to try and lay a glove or two on the undisputed world champions. In these days of fixture congestion, as each country tries to satisfy the increasing demands of the ICC calendar, it is noteworthy that the first five encounters between the two teams since their reacquaintance in 1994 have all been good old-fashioned, full-blooded five-match series.

The first of these during the English winter of 1995/96 was a cagey affair – broken up early on by the elements – which South Africa eventually won in a low-scoring final Test at Cape Town. For England the only valuable souvenir of the trip was Atherton's masterpiece of bloody-mindedness at the New Wanderers stadium in Johannesburg, as he laboured for almost eleven hours to save the Test. The English summer that split these first two rounds of the duel had seen Donald and Warwickshire reach their peak in the domestic game. The summer of 1995 confirmed the county as the dominant power in English cricket with a successful defence of their Championship title, victory in the NatWest Trophy and the Sunday League lost only on run rate. For Donald it was his most prolific year at the club and brought both professional and personal satisfaction.

The previous summer, while he was busy tormenting the English batsmen, a man with recent experience of giving their bowlers a merciless whipping was drafted in by Warwickshire as Donald's replacement. And instantly made a huge impression. Fresh from carting Messrs Fraser, Caddick, Tufnell and Lewis to all parts of the Recreation Ground in Antigua for a world record Test score of 375, Brian Charles Lara chose a County Championship fixture at Edgbaston as the scene for a fresh assault on the record pages of the golden almanack. 'I bet he goes on to score a hundred now.' This, legend has it, was the pep-talk Durham wicketkeeper Chris Scott delivered to his teammates shortly after grassing an offering from Lara's bat with his score on 18. The prediction proved to be wildly optimistic. As the sun dipped the following evening, record-breaking quintuple centurion Lara held his bat aloft in triumph, Scott – guilty of the costliest drop in cricket history – just held his head safely in his hands. Powered to their first Championship title since 1972 by the Trinidadian run machine, Warwickshire moved to secure a longer commitment from Lara, notwithstanding the availability of Donald. Despite the huge impact made by the West Indian when batting, his overall level of commitment was, at times, called into question. On one occasion he famously took a call on his mobile phone while fielding in the slips. This was a global superstar coping with the more prosaic realities of life on the relentless, often unglamorous county cricket circuit. Ultimately, he would decide against an immediate extension to his residency in the Midlands, returning several years later to captain a side which had, by then, slipped from the summit of English cricket.

When Donald retook his place at Edgbaston the following summer he was still smarting at the perceived lack of loyalty shown to him by the county he had served for seven years. He chose to channel his frustrations straight down the pitch at a succession of quivering batsmen. His 88 victims contributed massively to Warwickshire's successful defence of their Championship title. Concerned at the toll that year-round cricket was taking on his body (and a touch piqued by his employers' original preference for Lara), he elected to take a sabbatical during the 1996 summer, remaining at Edgbaston as a fitness coach and creating an opportunity in the side for his international teammate, Shaun Pollock. Rested and in peak condition, Donald embarked on a period of concentrated international competition. Between September 1996 and the return to England in 1998, South Africa's engagements included encounters at home and away with India, Australia and Pakistan – gathering wickets with a rhythmic consistency that eased him to the top of the ICC Test rankings.

From this lofty perch, Donald surveyed the challenging landscape that lay ahead. The five-match series against England in the summer of 1998 promised both a homecoming and the chance for redemption. Summers at Warwickshire had provided a glut of success and satisfaction, but his one previous Test series in England had left only a gnawing emptiness. The 1994 tour that had started so well, with the drubbing at Lord's, had ended in failure for his team at The Oval. Personal disappointment at the insinuation by his then captain that he had gone missing when the side required him most needed to be exorcised. The series would also provide an important measure of each country's standing in the global game. Both England and South Africa had flattered to deceive in their recent skirmishes with the Australians – starting with aggressive promise but succumbing to their opponent's superior talents and tougher core – and were eager to claim a victory to vindicate their assertions that genuine progress was being made.

The first Test at Edgbaston failed to deliver the glorious return Donald had hoped for as rain washed away the promise of a tight finish. But six wickets confirmed his form and a gem of a ball to remove Atherton (albeit after he had reached a century) presaged the personal contest that would underpin, illuminate and, more than any other, determine the outcome of the series. In the second Test the Proteas repeated their trick from the previous tour, dishing out a sound beating at Lord's as their hosts capitulated with the bat. Again Donald was the chief architect of their downfall, taking five wickets. He collected eight more in the next match as South African dominance continued at Old Trafford. England were forced to follow on for the second Test in succession, but – as in Johannesburg during the previous series – an epic rearguard from the skipper saved England. This time it was Alec Stewart. Batting for almost seven hours for 164, he ensured his side would remain just a single Test in arrears as they travelled to Nottingham. Desperate to retake the impetus in the series, the England selectors shuffled their pack, handing a recall to Hick, and adding something new in a first cap for

Andrew Flintoff. As England welcomed a brawny all-rounder into their side, the South Africans were driving theirs to the airport. With Procteresque shoulders and a similar penchant for beating the living daylights out of the ball, Lance Klusener had added crucial balance to the tourists' offensive operations. A usefully hostile bowler who supported the front-line surges of Donald and Pollock, with the bat he was – as many would discover to their cost the following summer as the World Cup came to England – a dangerous man to cross. Wielding a weapon the size of a railway sleeper he had taken to the English bowling like a duck to water, bludgeoning their offerings by land and air during a number of lively contributions late in the order. Now he was injured and out of the series.

At Trent Bridge the game began in a fairly orderly and undramatic fashion – after two innings their was little separating the sides – but once England had removed their hosts cheaply second time around to earn themselves a more than sporting chance of victory, all hell broke loose. In late afternoon sunshine Donald steamed into the crease from around the wicket and speared a ball across Atherton that flicked his batting glove on its way into the keeper's gauntlets. Out. The bowler raced towards his colleagues, euphoric that he had engineered the demise of England's most reliable asset. The rock, the hard place, too often the pain in their collective backsides – he was gone. Or was he? Suddenly Donald could see the jubilant grins in the slip cordon falling, to be replaced by grimaces of disbelief and disgust. Atherton was unmoved and so, crucially, was the umpire Steve Dunne. In his auto-biography Donald recalls the icy instruction he gave to the England opener as he returned to his mark, 'You'd better be fucking ready for what's coming.' And down it came – the works, the full beans, the kitchen sink – delivered with an intensity and fury that found its voice after each ball, as the bowler carried on down the pitch to hose Atherton down with a torrent of Anglo-Afrikaans invective. To make matters worse, the opener refused to rise. Stubborn as a mule but no ass, Atherton had long since worked out that a batsman who has time to engage in pithy badinage with the bowler, is a batsman whose mind is not entirely focussed on the task of protecting his wicket. He would speak to Donald – but in the dressing room, not in the middle – at the end of the following day's play in which he had finished unbeaten on 98 and England had drawn level in the series.

The series would finish in the same way as the 1994 meeting – England clambering off the canvas to catch their opponents with a sucker punch. In the final match at Headingley it was the turn of the South African batsmen to collapse like a house of cards – at one point they were 27/5 – leaving the all-rounders and bowlers to find the balance of a modest victory target. When it came, defeat in such a fashion was a particularly bitter pill for Donald, who earlier had left an

English cricket field for the final time as a Test bowler with eight wickets from the match and 33 in the series. England had secured their first series win against the new South Africa – it had hardly been convincing and at times questionable umpiring decisions had been crucial – but the ledger now balanced again. In three series played one was drawn and there was one victory apiece.

When the Proteas took their chance for revenge, as England made their fin de siecle tour to South Africa two years later, the two key players of the 1998 series enjoyed contrasting fortunes. Eleven wickets for Donald, and a pair for Atherton, in the first Test at Johannesburg exorcised the ghost of the latter's heroics on the same ground four years earlier and eased the home side to victory with an innings to spare. The series went the way of the home side, the following in England was drawn, the next encounter in South Africa belonged to the visitors. Three more series had resulted in one draw and one victory apiece.

For more than a decade, the sight of a tall, blonde figure marauding around English cricket grounds, the keen glint in his eyes illuminated by a thick daub of sunblock smeared across his nose and cheeks, was for some reassuring, for others terrifying. In either case their attention was commanded. To followers of Warwickshire County Cricket Club, Donald was the dynamic force driving their successful campaigns on all fronts during the early 1990s. For England fans he was too often the scourge of their batting line-up. Part of a golden generation of highly skilled assassins – McGrath, Walsh and Ambrose, Wasim and Waqar – that were wonderful to behold but pretty ghastly to face, his lines of attack were murderous yet thoughtful, messing up the batsmen's mind as well as his body. At a time when success in English cricket was often measured by the grittiness of the rearguards they mounted against superior opposition, the battles that raged between Donald and Atherton defined the war for supremacy waged between England and South Africa. The seminal image of this rivalry shows Donald passing Atherton mid-pitch at Trent Bridge at the height of their duel in 1998. The hatred in his eyes looks pretty genuine. But after the dust settled the two men had compared their understanding of the realities of the professional game over the proverbial 'beer afterwards' – sometimes you get the rub of the green, batsmen only walk when their cars run out of petrol, umpires are only human, that sort of thing – but most of all they shared a respect for the skills and competitive instincts of the other. They also knew that when they next took to the field, trophies and accolades would be up for grabs but, in reality, at least in their lives as professional sportsmen, that half hour spent out in the middle at Trent Bridge as the sun dipped on Sunday evening was just about as good as it would ever, could ever, possibly get.

TWELVE

THE PATRON SAINT
OF LOST CAUSES

'We flippin' murdered 'em. Hammered them. Bloody steamrollered them. They know it and we know it.' It is December 1996 and, as the sun sets on the Queens Club in Bulawayo, England's coach David Lloyd is sharing his views on the inaugural Test match between Zimbabwe and England with the gentlemen of the press. While the reports they would file for their newspapers focussed on Lloyd's fruity post-match outburst, they also recorded another salient point, absent from his review of the fixture – the match had ended in a flippin' draw.

As is often the case in sport, the result tells less than half the story. An evenly balanced contest between bat and ball over the first four days, the fifth brought mayhem. It all began when the final Zimbabwean wicket fell, dangling a tantalising target of 205 from 37 overs in front of the tourists. As they took to the field their hosts were still smarting at the exuberance and frequency of the England appealing earlier in the day – the match referee Hanumant Singh later issued a public warning – and took a pragmatic approach to close out the game. Their tactics during the closing sessions of the contest – bowling wide to far-flung fields – left the English batsmen stranded, one run shy of their victory target, and their team coach spluttering irately about murder, hammers and steam.

Given time for quiet reflection Lloyd and his team would no doubt have identified the key moments during the game (aside from that frustrated run chase) when victory slipped from their grasp. The second morning, for example. Coming out to bowl at their hosts with the top order already safely back in the pavilion, England's plan would have involved a clatter of early wickets, followed by the construction of a substantial first-innings lead. What they got was another long day in the field and ringside seats at a masterclass in batting with the lower order from a man with a habit of raising his game when all appeared lost.

Andy Flower had celebrated his country's first international match four years earlier with a century against Sri Lanka and their first Test victory with a captain's innings of 156 against Pakistan; it was little wonder that he would mark the occasion of England's first visit with another century. The only surprise, perhaps, was that he chose to reach the landmark with the aid of a reverse sweep. In many ways that innings in Bulawayo provided a microcosm of Flower's international career, a calm, highly skilled performance against the odds that elevated his team to better things.

With the remaining Test in Harare an unresolved wash-out, England returned to the Sports Club on New Year's Day for the second match in the one-day series looking to salvage something useful from the tour. The first one-day game had gone the way of the home side, when England crumbled to 152 all out. Batting first in the second game Zimbabwe made an even 200, with Flower again holding things together just as they were threatening to unravel with a watchful 63 assembled in just under three hours that steadied the ship. His contribution behind the stumps ensured that England's progress towards victory staggered and ultimately fell, catching the in-form Stewart and stumping first Crawley and then a future Essex teammate in Ronnie Irani.

Zimbabwe had completed their first success in a one-day series and England's misery was complete. Well, almost. The final match in the series, now a dead rubber, saw the local heroes triumph again to screw the lid onto a 3-0 victory. Once again Flower was a key figure, adding impetus to the mid-section of the innings, before pouching a quintet of catches behind the stumps – with four coming off the bowling of Eddo Brandes. Brandes completed a hat-trick in the process, thereby securing a second entry in the annals of cricket history. The rotund chicken farmer's main claim to fame will always be as the man who sent a sledge worthy of the Cresta Run straight back at the Australians. When Glenn McGrath queried why Brandes was so generously proportioned, the Zimbabwean didn't miss a beat in retorting: 'Because every time I fuck your wife she gives me a biscuit'.

While the tour may have represented a low point for English cricket, it marked a redemption of sorts for Flower. Earlier in the year he had resigned the captaincy, bowing to the strain of multi-tasking the disciplines of batting, keeping and leading. By the time that Zimbabwe arrived in England for the World Cup three years later, their hosts had been grappling with a similar quandary for some time – ultimately casting Alec Stewart in the role of jack-of-all-trades. Although Stewart's team prevailed when the two sides met at Trent Bridge early in the tournament, it would be the Zimbabweans that progressed to the Super Sixes, leaving the home side stranded at the group stage, surrounded by questions and recriminations. For English cricket in the 1990s, when sorrows came they came not by single spies but in battalions. The World Cup failure was followed by a first home Test series defeat to New Zealand which, in turn, preceded a 2-1 reversal in South Africa. Although history will always remember the final Test of that series against the Proteas for reasons other than sport – Hansie Cronje's apparent largesse in offering to forfeit an innings in a rain-soaked match was later re-examined in the light of match-fixing allegations – victory at Centurion Park represented a significant turning point for the England team. A quiet revolution was underway. Its aim was to make 'Team England' a sharper, tougher more adaptable unit. Its architect was the former Zimbabwean international Duncan Fletcher.

As it turned out, England's new resolve was more luxury than necessity in the first match of the following summer. With Andy Flower once again leading the side the Zimbabweans arrived at Lord's ill-prepared for their first Tests on English soil. The news from home was not good – farmlands were coming under increasing threat from squatters, while the growing sense of instability had sent the dollar into free-fall. If the anxieties over the well-being of their families were not enough to distract the players, their relative poverty was. One member of the squad was reprimanded by the Zimbabwe Cricket Union for leaking to the press the damning news that the highest-paid member of the touring party was the bloke driving the bus. To add to their lost earnings the team was also missing a tenor. Opera-singing fast-bowler Henry Olonga, whose flailing dreadlocks and dazzling grin had caught the eye in England during the previous summer's World Cup, was unavailable through injury.

Against this backdrop it is perhaps unsurprising that the visitors broke with the tradition of dishing out a hiding to their hosts at Lord's in favour of a spectacular capitulation. Even with rain delays, the game – it was neither a test nor a match – was over in three-and-a-half days. The final act

– Pommy Mbangwa nodding a rising delivery from Andy Caddick deftly down onto his stumps – provided a tragicomic finale. Reflecting on England's victory by an innings and 209 runs, the post-match reactions of the two captains were, by turns, predictable and prescient. Flower urged his men to take a 'harsh look' at themselves; Hussain spoke of the need to guard against a 'wounded' foe.

Victories for the tourists over Yorkshire and the MCC before the second and final Test went some way to rebuilding their confidence. They arrived in Nottingham with renewed optimism and a point to prove. Had it not been for the rain, they might well have surpassed this aspiration and snatched an improbable victory to level the series. Their positive intentions became clear when Flower declared his first innings after only their fourth wicket had fallen, with his side still 89 runs adrift of England's total. This spirited gesture was possible thanks to the solid productivity of the middle order. Both Neil Johnson and Flower himself sharing century partnerships with Murray Goodwin who finished unbeaten on 148. It is no surprise that all three would later find employment with English county sides. It may have been that the overnight declaration took England by surprise, or possibly the Zimbabwean bowlers drew inspiration from the performance of their batting colleagues the previous day. Perhaps it was the absence of Mike Atherton from the top order. England's centurion from the first innings, laid low with a stomach bug, produced a different sort of gutsy performance and was relegated to an appearance at no.7. Whatever the underlying reasons, England got off to the opposite of 'a flyer'. By the time that the opening odd-couple of Ramprakash and Knight had been separated and then reunited in the pavilion, Hussain was already there trying not look at a scoreboard that read 12/3. Hick, Stewart and Flintoff all got started before edging their way into Flower's gloves. Atherton rose like Lazarus to partner the tail, but by the time that Caddick had become the keeper's fifth victim and Gough had given Guy Whittall his fiftieth Test wicket, England were all out for 147.

In contrast to the farrago of controversy served up on that infamous final afternoon in Bulawayo four years earlier, Zimbabwe's 'target' of 237 from 13 overs was sufficiently implausible to raise anyone's blood pressure. Although the batsmen came out looking ready for business, by the time that Nasser Hussain had chucked the ball to Mark Ramprakash to take over from Darren Gough at the Pavilion End, it was clear that the game was up. A draw was recorded in the scorebook; a moral victory was declared for the away side.

At the risk of sounding like the narrator of a Hovis commercial, I can remember when a summer of international cricket simply involved England taking on another country in a Test and one-day series. With the ICC family expanding, and the commercial possibilities of the one-day game becoming more apparent, times have changed. Take the summer of 2005: England played a mini-Test series against Bangladesh, a Twenty20 international against Australia, a triangular one-day series with both, plus a further one-day series against Australia. Oh, and the Ashes. Despite various positive outcomes – international cricket travels the country, emerging sides receive useful experience and exposure, the odd tremendous upset occurs (see Australia *v.* Bangladesh, 2005) – critics argue that the quality is increasingly lost in the quantity, that too many games are meaningless and mismatches are all too frequent.

When the West Indies arrived for the latter half of the summer of 2000, many assumed that there would be only two teams in the NatWest triangular tournament. Indeed there were, England and Zimbabwe. Heartened by their performance in the second Test, Flower's men started the series on what is referred to in sprinting circles as the 'b' of the bang. They beat the West Indies with ease at Bristol before heading down to The Oval to see off England.

It has become fashionable to refer to teams that underperform during the early part of tours as being 'under-cooked'; in July 2000 the men from the Caribbean looked raw. The Zimbabweans strolled past them at Canterbury; they then collapsed against England at Chester-le-Street without claiming a single wicket before losing out in a closer encounter with Zimbabwe at the same venue. Although the final at Lord's went England's way, with Alec Stewart following centuries in his previous two innings with a match-winning 97, both England and Zimbabwe had made subtle yet significant progress since their meeting on the same ground earlier in the summer. Having provided meagre resistance in that first Test, in the games that followed the African tourists had taught their hosts a lesson or two about tough cricket. England would draw on this experience, and the talents of a new crop of players – Vaughan, Trescothick, Flintoff – to come from behind to secure a cathartic victory over the West Indies in the second Test series of the summer. Success during the winter against Sri Lanka and Pakistan provided further proof that English cricket was sloughing off the dead skin of mediocrity that it had worn for much of the previous decade.

For Zimbabwe, success on the sports field had greater implications, evidenced by the response of Morgan Tsvangirai, president of the Movement for Democratic Change, to the team's progress to the NatWest final: 'This success brings some sense of normality to Zimbabweans at home, which is very important in these turbulent times. I salute their dedication and commitment, which reflects on our culture, here at home.' The reality of the lack of normality in Zimbabwe was evident in Flower's demotion as captain, shortly after the English tour, to be replaced by Heath Streak, whose father was a recent appointment to the selection panel.

Although cricketers have not, as yet, embraced the culture of body art with the same gusto as their colleagues from the soccer world, I would suggest that if Andy Flower were to consider a tattoo he could do worse than Friedrich Nietzsche's musing: 'What does not destroy me, makes me stronger.' His response to losing the captaincy was to produce a string of performances, during the following two years, that would have guaranteed him a place in any team in the world. In the nine Tests that followed his demotion he scored over 1,000 runs at a shade under ninety. The Indians bore the brunt as Flower hit his straps. His return against them from the four innings of a two-Test series was 183 not out, 70, 55 and 232 not out. To borrow a phrase from the over-stocked cupboard of footballing cliché, the lad was on fire. The South Africans also got burnt the following season in Harare, as Flower followed a century in the first innings with an unbeaten 199 in the second to leapfrog Steve Waugh and Sachin Tendulkar to the top of the ICC ratings. The former skipper had soon collected further titles as the Federation of International Cricketers Association, *Wisden* and his country all recognised him as their man of the year.

If Flower and England had emerged revitalised and reborn from their engagements in 2000 their meeting scheduled for 13 February 2003, signalled the beginning of the end for the former and the end of the beginning for the latter. Ahead of the fixture in question – a World Cup pool match in Harare – the England camp was in turmoil. Aside from the security issues associated with travelling to Zimbabwe, the chief concern occupying the players and administrators was that their participation in the game would cast them as the unwilling support act in a political sideshow. More specifically, Robert Mugabe's view that, 'cricket civilizes people and creates good gentlemen' presaged a photograph opportunity before the game: a gentlemanly handshake between the president and the England captain, for example. The acronyms went to war as the ECB wanted the game moved to South Africa; the ICC did not; the ZCU made noises about compensation if England failed to honour the fixture. No one emerged with conspicuous credit, but Zimbabwe took the points that, by default, cost England a place in the final stages of the tournament.

Wearied by the whole wretched business, Nasser Hussain stepped down as captain of the one-day side. In an emotional signing-off press conference he referred to his desire to 'go back to doing what I wanted to do as a boy: to play Test cricket for England, not be a national spokesman for everything cricketing'. Later that year, his successor at the helm of the one-day team, Michael Vaughan, would also inherit from Hussain the responsibility for leading the Test team. Phase one of the Fletcher revolution reached its conclusion over the Harare fiasco, phase two – stand by for record-breaking victories and Ashes redemption – was just beginning.

As England vacillated over the political implications of playing the match, Flower was already taking decisive steps. On the morning of Zimbabwe's opening match against

Namibia he issued a statement, together with Henry Olonga, explaining that they could not, 'in good conscience take to the field and ignore the fact that millions of our compatriots are starving, unemployed and oppressed.' They also stated that their decision to wear black armbands on the field of play was in mourning for 'the death of democracy in our beloved Zimbabwe' and represented a 'silent plea to those responsible to stop the abuse of human rights in Zimbabwe.' Unsurprisingly their actions were met with condemnation within Zimbabwe and admiration everywhere else. Equally predictable was Flower's retirement from international cricket at the end of the tournament and exile from his homeland.

As with many of the stories described in this book, one country's loss results in palpable gains for English cricket. In the summer preceding the World Cup, Flower had completed a successful first summer with Essex, scoring more than 1,000 runs at over fifty in their victorious campaign in the Championship second division. Over the next four seasons he never failed to score less than 1,000 runs, averaging over seventy for his final two summers. As a senior player and qualified coach, his work at Essex aiding the development of the county's younger talent did not go unnoticed. When England were slammed back to earth with their 5-0 Ashes reversal in the winter of 2006/07, Duncan Fletcher's time was up. But the ECB moved swiftly to appoint Flower as an assistant coach in a team charged with rediscovering the winning formula in time for the next clash in England during the summer of 2009. The omens look promising. The last man to coach England to Ashes victory also hailed from Zimbabwe and, as *Wisden* pointed out, Flower has spent much of his cricketing life as the Patron Saint of Lost Causes.

THIRTEEN

NUTS ABOUT KP

When the American comedian and actor Robin Williams described cricket as 'baseball on valium' he was not, to borrow from the lexicon of marketing, comparing apples with apples. Broadly speaking there is little common ground between the muddy, attritional, often low-scoring contests found in British sport and the Hollywoodesque hoopla of the American offerings, where drama and commerce are squeezed into and out of every play. We have a combative, dour Merseyside derby settled in the eighty-ninth minute by a dodgy penalty. They have a scrimmage in the end-zone in the final seconds of the fourth quarter and a washed-up former legend, called up from the bench to throw one last Hail Mary pass… but first, a message from our sponsors. Notwithstanding the evolution of Test matches, through the pyjama and floodlights revolution of one-day games, into the hectic slogfest of Twenty20, cricket remains the farthest removed from the American ideal. Take the Atherton/ Donald ding-dong from 1998, no wickets fell, barely a run was scored, it was without a doubt one of the most compelling passages of play ever seen on a cricket field. This subtlety in the exposition of drama can of course be a double-edged sword. When, in the early evening of 12 September 2005 a seismic event shuddered through the core of English sport (indeed through the national consciousness) its dramatic enactment involved two middle-aged men ambling into the centre of a deserted pitch to each ceremoniously flick a pair of small, lathed tubes of wood onto the floor.

If not the 'greatest ever series' so named by a local media intoxicated with patriotism, the 2005 Ashes was undoubtedly a classic – delivering giddy highs and gut-wrenching lows from start to finish. Well almost. When the umpires removed the bails to signify the end there was an inevitable sense of anticlimax, Flintoff heaving a Warne delivery into the stand to find the six runs needed for victory from the final ball would have been better. But, at least, for most of the final day, the drama had been suffocatingly intense. At the end of a long summer of toil and tension, England were threatening to snatch defeat from the jaws of victory. Going into the finale at The Oval 2-1 up in the series, only a draw was needed to secure a cathartic victory – the Ashes had sat in Australian hands for a decade and a half – and confirm the status of Michael Vaughan's team as genuine pretenders to the throne of world cricket. But at lunch on the final day it looked pretty bleak. Many runs from safety with all but one of the top six back in the pavilion, there was enough time for the Australians to grab the necessary runs and turn the water cannon on England's parade. The balance between heroic success and sickening failure was thus set; at its fulcrum stood a young man from KwaZulu-Natal, boasting a faintly ludicrous hairdo and, of more relevance to the outcome of the match, balls of steel. In many ways the former was simply proof of the latter; proof of a self-belief and single-mindedness that had taken Kevin Pietersen to the summit of English cricket.

He was raised with three brothers in a household ruled by the twin religions of sport and Christianity. Under the watchful eye of a father unafraid to wield a cane, even as a schoolboy Pietersen's competitive edge was sharp enough to earn him provincial colours in swimming, cross-country, squash, rugby and cricket. It was, of course, the last of these that would claim his full attention but his early inclinations favoured the ball over the bat as he developed into a useful off-spinner capable of adding runs in the middle order. By the time that Nasser Hussain took England to South Africa in 1999/2000, Pietersen had found his place in the KwaZulu-Natal first team and made an instant impression on the tourists, scoring an unbeaten 61 at no.9 and collecting four wickets with Atherton, Hussain and Vaughan among them.

Already weighing up the options offered by his English mother and a British passport, Pietersen sought Hussain out after the game to enquire about the possibility of employment in the county game. But it would be another Hussain that would shape his cricketing destiny. When Goolam Hussain Bodi – another off-spinner-batsman – took Pietersen's place in the KwaZulu-Natal side, he took decisive action. Stung by the notion that he was a victim of the racial quota system requiring each province to field a prescribed number of non-white players, Pietersen sought counsel. First with the management at KwaZulu-Natal, then with Dr Ali Bacher, but perhaps most significantly with Clive Rice. Rice had been following Pietersen's progress ever since he had chosen him for the South African Schools side. Rice, who had shown impeccable judgement, timing and motivational skills while captain of Nottinghamshire now relied on these qualities as their coach. Dropped by KwaZulu-Natal, Pietersen was left with an empty feeling; doubts could have crept in but Rice soon filled the void. The young man was told he was a great player; he would be a star in county cricket and in four years he would be playing for England.

Although Rice's prediction would ultimately be proved accurate, Pietersen would spend the greater part of his four-year qualification period at Nottinghamshire without the guiding hand of his compatriot on his shoulder. Following a successful debut season at Trent Bridge as more than 1,000 runs at over fifty elevated him to the top of the county's first-class averages, a position he would not relinquish during his four summers at Trent Bridge – the second season was fraught with difficulty and disappointment. Already aggrieved at the manner of Rice's departure from the East Midlands, Pietersen took an instant dislike to the replacement coach Mike Newell. Having lionised Rice as the archetypal South African sportsman – competitive, tough and results-focussed – Pietersen saw in Newell the worst of English county cricket: mediocrity, comfort, lack of a cutting edge. The nascent relationship between aspiring Test player and new coach was not helped when shortly after his appointment Newell dropped Pietersen to the Second XI.

Irritated at the perceived need to prove himself afresh, Pietersen's response on his return to first-team duty was emphatic, as four successive centuries confirmed his status as one of the best young batsmen in the country. Although Nottinghamshire would finish the season on a high with promotion to the first division, after his hot streak earlier in the summer injury cast Pietersen as a somewhat peripheral figure. The following season the fortunes of player and club diverged. Pietersen made a near 1,500 runs at 51 in first-class matches, and his 776 runs in one-day cricket supported a claim for international recognition. His team, however, struggled with the pace in the upper tier of the domestic game and had soon slumped back down to the second division. More significantly,

Pietersen's third summer at Trent Bridge represented the nadir of his relationship with the establishment and management at the club. As the season played out and frustrations grew at Nottinghamshire's southerly slide down the table, Pietersen was openly critical of the coach and the captain Jason Gallian. Eventually, during a team meeting at which Pietersen was not present, Gallian snapped and heaved his absent colleague's kit bag over the dressing room balcony, a crudely symbolic gesture that led the South African to consider breaking his contract with the county a year early. Pietersen stayed but his focus was now sharpened on the main prize.

The winter that followed his summer of discontent brought him a step closer. Selected to attend the England Academy he instantly responded to the approach and style of its director, the former Australian Test wicketkeeper Rod Marsh. Bristling behind a bushy moustache, Marsh, like Clive Rice, personified the south-of-the-Equator sporting ethic: work hard in the gym, play hard on the pitch. Pietersen flourished at the academy, putting theory into practice with four centuries and a ninety as the 'course' culminated in a tour to India. His successes reassured the selectors on two counts. With the bat his was a talent impossible to ignore and his attitude and temperament – under close scrutiny following the difficulties at Nottinghamshire – had also proved reliable, both on and off the pitch. Like Hick a decade and a half earlier, the whispering campaign was by now well underway. This South African diamond might not be flawless but he looked set to lend some sparkle to English cricket for many years to come.

Emerging from the tensions of the previous season, Pietersen's final summer at Trent Bridge brought success for both player and club. Promotion back to top tier of domestic cricket provided a springboard for the county from which they would secure their first Championship title since Rice's swansong in 1987. A defining factor was the astute acquisition of the New Zealander Stephen Fleming, the shrewdest captain in world cricket and an elegantly effective batsmen, to lead the side. For Pietersen, another productive year with the willow saw him depart Nottinghamshire carrying with him sixteen first-class centuries and an average in excess of fifty-five. Having seen a tall, powerful strokemaker from Natal star in the late 1960s and 1970s, followers of Hampshire County Cricket Club would now be treated to a repeat performance, as Pietersen chose the South Coast as the location for the next chapter in his adventures in county cricket. It is no coincidence that the dominant personality at Hampshire, a certain Mr Shane Warne, their captain, was a tough and aggressive, hugely experienced and respected international cricketer. Precisely the kind of character that Pietersen had previously sought out as mentors.

The winter that preceded his arrival on the South Coast secured Pietersen's fate as the saviour that England would turn to in the summer that followed, when the most eagerly anticipated Ashes battle for many years was joined. It began with a tour to Zimbabwe and a one-day series against a side struggling to cope with the demands of international sport, while political turmoil continued to ravage their country. For Pietersen the tour represented a gentle baptism into international cricket. But the chrism would soon enough turn to paraffin for his next engagement in England colours, a return to South Africa, and the promise of some real fireworks.

When expressed collectively, the critical faculties of a stadium full of over-hyped and often beered-up supporters will invariably deploy wit as a bludgeon rather than as a rapier. We're back to heroes and villains, goodies and baddies and nothing in between. A football crowd, for example, will tend to chastise their prey by degrees. A less than svelte player, wheezing through the early season skirmishes, will be damned for his evident rapacity where pies are concerned. The poor soul off-loaded by a rival club will have 'fucking reject' bellowed at them for ninety minutes. But the cardinal sin is committed by the player returning to their former club in the colours of an opponent, having departed under a cloud. A handful of years before Pietersen returned to South Africa, an English Premier League fixture provided the classic example of the last of these torments. The venue was White Hart Lane and the centre of attention was Sulzeer Jeremiah Campbell. 'Sol' had left Tottenham Hotpsur for their arch, local rivals Arsenal in search of heightened glories, which instantly arrived. But on his first return to the club he had grown up with, the vilification from the home fans was bitterly intense. In the days before the match the following, somewhat bizarre, transaction must have taken place, somewhere in North London. A customer walks into a party accessories shop and orders several thousand balloons for the following Saturday. The proprietor replies, 'Certainly sir, and the message? "Congratulations you're 3?", "Happy retirement?", "Bon voyage?"' 'No,' replies the customer, 'just put "Judas" please.'

When Pietersen strode out at the New Wanderers Stadium in Johannesburg on 30 January 2005, wearing the blue and red colours of England, the reception was mixed. Some booed, others jeered, many shouted, 'Judas'. He stuck around until the end of the innings to guide the side home, and now the game was on. The second match was in Bloemfontein, the farming heartland of conservative, meat-eating, rugby-worshipping South Africa. The game finished in an improbable tie, but Pietersen grabbed the headlines with a dashing century, welcomed by its architect with a kiss of the badge on his helmet, and by the crowd with a collective, symbolic, turning of their backs. Following defeat at Port Elizabeth, England travelled to Cape Town where, perhaps subconsciously aware of his growing marketability, Pietersen made his first foray into the spangly world of the ostentatiously eye-catching coiffure. Crowned with a copper-tinted

homage to road-kill he endeared himself even less to the
home crowds with a rakish 75 from 85 balls.

Although England effectively lost the series in the next
match at East London, for Pietersen an innings of 100 runs
scored from 69 balls – the fastest century by an English player
in a one-day international – sealed with a six from the last
ball of the match, confirmed his status as the new talisman of
English cricket. Twenty years earlier Ian Botham had sauntered to the crease at Edgbaston, sporting a hairdo flamboyant
even for the 1980s and struck the first ball he received into
the stand. That final ball, arcing across the night sky in East
London, effectively launched the KP brand. Another century
in the final game of the series added further to his burgeon-
ing myth – as did the numbers he carried aboard the plane
back to England – 454 runs from six innings at a tidy average
of 151 – and even elicited applause from the home crowd.
He had crossed the Rubicon and reached the bank on the
other side a hero. Ever the modern sportsman, the three lions
tattooed onto his bicep in a shopping mall in Johannesburg
shortly before departing marked the occasion in style.

Hindsight makes geniuses of us all. Viewed through the
smoking wreckage of England's latest tour to Australia, their
2005 Ashes triumph appears not as the sturdy template for
future success but rather a flighty, ephemeral glimpse of
sporting perfection. But watching the open-top bus parade
edging through central London in bright, early autumn

sunshine it was tempting to believe the hype. The unruly rabble grinning down at us from the top deck would be the generation that would re-balance the dreadfully one-sided contest that the Ashes had become, while the tormentors of the past decade – Warne, McGrath, Hayden et al – slunk off quietly into retirement, defeated. No, not terribly plausible is it? In reality Australia's old guard stirred themselves for decisive retribution in 2006/07, while many of the pillars of England's success from 2005 – Trescothick, Vaughan, Flintoff, Simon Jones, Harmison – crumbled into a dust of injury and lost form.

One of the few England players to excel in both series, Pietersen was not even in the Test side when the Australians arrived in the early summer of 2005. With five straight series victories behind them Vaughan's XI was a closed shop. The only daylight appeared in the top-order where Ian Bell – a prospect fancied by many to pick up Atherton's burden as the trusty accumulator – replaced the more dashing Robert Key. And that appeared to be that. But as with Hick fourteen years earlier, Pietersen had been busy fuelling expectations and dreams. His successes in South Africa had confirmed his ability to produce performances of the highest quality under extreme pressure; his eye-catching contributions during the one-day games early in the summer furthered his Ashes cause. Aggressive, unpredictable, a winner; to jumble a metaphor from the world of Italian football, here was a man to fulfil the dual roles of *Fantasista* and *Salvatore*. So when Graham Thorpe – a key figure in the settled batting order, enjoying a golden autumn to his Test career – added the announcement of his unavailability for the next winter tour due to lurking doubts over his troublesome back, KP was in like a shot.

As ever, selectorial judgement divided opinion. While for many Pietersen personified the 'they don't like it up 'em' style needed to wrest the Ashes from Australian grasp, others valued the Test match experience offered by Thorpe's decade-long residence in the trenches. The latter camp argued that if England found themselves at say 18/3 in their first innings, in the first Test, Thorpe would be best equipped for hauling the side out of the bog. We can safely assume then that when Pietersen emerged from the pavilion at Lord's for his debut Test innings with England sinking at 18/3, the selectors, to a man, edged forward in their seats. They would watch a young man playing the match situation rather than to the tune of the tumult of hype that accompanied his march to the middle. Applying the D'Oliveira technique, he took a long hard look at the bowling of McGrath and Warne before trying anything flighty. When he did, by clubbing errant offerings from each of these legends into the less reasonably priced seating in the upper tiers, the crowd came alive. But despite these high points, the sinking feeling sweeping Lord's by Sunday afternoon was all-too familiar; England were going down to Australia by a dispiriting margin. Any dreams of Ashes reclamation were clearly just that.

The second Test – agreed by many to be one of the finest ever played – emphasised the value of the two key talents of the series. In the red and white corner, Flintoff's muscular and inspirational displays made him the first genuine contender to adequately fill the long-vacant 'Next Botham' title. Dancing out of the green and gold corner, Warne added some hearty batting to his usual brilliance with the ball. As the series ebbed and flowed, one way then the other, it was these two men that would invariably come to the aid of their team, digging deep for advantage, paddling against the tide drawing them down a certain creek. Ultimately it would be Flintoff's timely interventions with bat and ball that secured the victory at Edgbaston to draw England level, but not before a gut-wrenching passage of play on the Sunday morning had brought the nation to its knees, fearing the worst. Deliverance came at the death. Harmison loped in, Kasprowicz fenced, behind the stumps Geraint Jones tumbled forward and pouched the catch. The England players went wild, the crowd erupted, at home the viewing audience emerged from behind the sofa. Now England truly believed. If this was the match that, more than any other, displayed England's new found confidence and purpose, then the crucial marker was laid down on the first afternoon as Flintoff and Pietersen passed a jolly hour battering the Australian bowling to all parts of a raucous Edgbaston. English cricket fans had not had this much fun since Graham Dilley wandered out to the middle at Headingley in 1981, to be greeted by Ian Botham's incisive analysis of the impending situation: 'Come on then, let's give it some humpty.'

With the series level, England travelled to Old Trafford a few days later exhilarated and confident. But one of the few questions gnawing at their newfound certainty concerned the batting form of the skipper. Lauded for his near faultless tactical judgement, Michael Vaughan's lean run of scores brought mutterings within the English media and hope for the Australian camp. The pre-eminent English batsmen of the previous Ashes, Vaughan had set altitudinous standards on Australian soil while his teammates had struggled around him. At Old Trafford, to borrow a favourite cliché of England's then-coach Duncan Fletcher, the captain 'came to the party.' Not so much blundering in through the kitchen door clutching a six pack of tinnies, as gliding onto a yacht in black tie, sipping a cocktail. Like Gower before him, when Vaughan came to the party he did so in style. As an England cricket fan, there are few more aesthetically pleasing sights than Vaughan caressing the ball through the covers. The pyrotechnics served up by Flintoff and Pietersen at Edgbaston had punched a few holes in the Australian confidence with the iron fist, now they were getting slapped about by the velvet glove. The captain's epic 166 painted the tourists into a corner from day one, and it was only an equally brilliant century from their skipper – a masterpiece of resilience, concentration and pacing from Ponting – that saved them on the final day.

The series moved on to Trent Bridge but the initiative stayed with England. Vaughan made a point of drawing his charges' attention to the vigour with which the previously insuperable Australians had celebrated their narrow escape in Lancashire. In Nottingham, Flintoff again took centre stage with a measured century in a game dominated by the bowlers. Having made Australia follow-on, England's victory target of 126 was modest, dangerously so. Following the kind of perverse logic that gives sport its endless appeal, Test sides have often sweated more profusely over the smaller totals than the larger ones. It's the underdog psychology reversed. Teams unburdened by genuine hope tend to play above themselves, while those carrying the weighty expectation of a stroll to glory have shown a tendency to stumble. When Flintoff and Pietersen were together, batting with some care, for three-quarters of an hour on the Sunday afternoon, all was well, the 100 came up leaving a paltry twenty-nine left to find. But then it all went horribly wrong. A man soon to be celebrated for allowing valour to overcome discretion, Pietersen suddenly lost his head, flayed at a wide ball from Lee and was caught behind. When the same bowler cleaned up Flintoff and Warne had coaxed Geraint Jones into an ill-advised lofted drive, the colour began to drain from the faces on the England balcony. In a summer littered with unforgettable images, the Trent Bridge Test produced several iconic scenes such as the Andrew Strauss 'Superman' catch to remove Gilchrist and the icy rage pinching Ponting's features as he mouthed to the England balcony having been run out by a substitute fielder among them. But perhaps the seminal shot captures Matthew Hoggard, the perennial nightwatchman, the blockmeister, England's minister of defence, eyes wide with concentration (or perhaps disbelief), stroking a glorious off-drive from the bowling of Lee for the boundary that would dispel any remaining doubt.

For all the dash and verve that Pietersen brought to the England cause with his batting during the summer, one aspect of his game had been spectacularly deficient. A normally reliable and athletic fielder, during the first four Tests he had approached the task of catching the ball with all the aplomb of a three-year-old wearing unlaced boxing gloves attempting to juggle a bar of soap. Time and again the ball glanced off Antipodean willow, only to cannon off his palms and hit the dirt, earning him the nickname 'cymbals' from the ever-inventive Australian sledging team. Ironically it was a song title from the Australian band Butterfingers that would provide the opposition with an alias for Pietersen during the return match Down Under, the acronymic 'Figjam' ('Fuck I'm good, just ask me'). His final innings of the 2005 series would present Pietersen with a karmic revenge over those who had mocked his earlier drops. Brooding skies over The Oval had broken up the early exchanges in the crucial final Test, but when the sun came out on the final day the equation was simple enough. England needed to bat for most of it to walk away with the Ashes.

By the time that Pietersen arrived at the crease they were staggering rather than striding to the finish line. Three wickets were down before lunch with McGrath on a hat-trick. Surviving the raucous appeal that greeted his first ball was only the beginning for England's fifth man in. A tentative prod at Warne brushed Gilchrist's gloves only to be spilled by Hayden at slip. Sinned against then turned sinner as Warne took his place in the cordon and grassed another chance, this time off the bowling of Brett Lee. The Australians had reimbursed Pietersen for his largesse earlier in the summer, now he would make them pay. If Botham's 'humpty' call-to-arms at Headingley in 1981 had stopped some way short of the St Crispin's day address, Pietersen's comment to Marcus Trescothick, shortly before lunch at The Oval in 2005, cut to the chase with even less ceremony: 'I'm just going to whack it now.'

Under mounting pressure, faced with the stiffest competition, the coaching, the sports psychology, the conditioning that makes up the modern sporting icon were cast aside in favour of an instinctive, reactive response. Pietersen was back in the garden, facing an older brother tying to knock his block off. If the ball was in reach, he was just going to whack it. Fair play. A brace of sixes off the bowling of Warne set the tempo, but the clatter of wickets at the other end – England were five down at lunch – kept the home support writhing in anguish and uncertainty. The duel between Lee and Pietersen either side of the interval proved decisive. Having ducked and dived in the face of a barrage of short-pitched bullets early in his innings, Pietersen returned after the break clearly set on both fight and flight. If a near-100mph delivery reared at him, he simply redirected its trajectory heavenward, up and away into a delirious crowd. And then he did it again. And again. The sun shone, the Ashes teetered in the balance, Australia's fastest bowler tore in like a dervish and England's last hope flayed the ball recklessly to all parts of the ground. Baseball on valium? This was cricket on ecstasy.

Over the course of the summer of 2005, England won the Ashes through collective resilience and individual brilliance, but without Pietersen's century in that final play, it would have more than likely been Ricky Ponting holding aloft the urn as the evening sunlight dipped on The Oval. Pietersen's subsequent exploits in a relatively brief Test career have confirmed the talent, temperament and potential of the young man described by Nasser Hussain as a 'champion' following the crucial innings that secured the Ashes. Even as England were being emphatically beaten in the return match eighteen months later, a series of dominant performances from Pietersen still commanded the respect of the victors.

It was a respect worth earning. For all the rhetoric and sabre rattling that accompanied the 2005 result, it would soon enough become clear that Australia remain the dominant force in world cricket. Vaughan's men did not suddenly assume that mantle on that September evening at The Oval – but their achievement was almost as significant. Eighteen years of one-sided Ashes series had devalued the contest and, regular as clockwork, every two years, subdued and dispirited English cricket. Pietersen's timely intervention broke the cycle – the game shook off its biannual season of hand-wringing and introspection to bask in the glow of an exciting and deeply satisfying triumph.

The venue at which – according to the famous mock obituary from *The Sporting Times* – English cricket 'died' in 1882 has seen many life-affirming sporting moments since that infamous occasion. Few who witnessed it will forget the time that a South African wearing the colours of England walked out to the middle of The Oval to face the Australians, carrying with him a hefty burden of pressure and expectation. Now he began tentatively but, backing his technique and natural ability, survived and prevailed in the most spectacular fashion, scoring a century to change the course of English cricketing history. D'Oliveira and Pietersen, two gifted sportsmen pursuing their careers on foreign soil – superficially for the same reason, but under markedly different circumstances – playing the innings of their life. Two men, thirty-seven years apart, with 158 runs apiece left their indelible imprint on our enduring national summer pastime of cricket: that endlessly fascinating, beautifully intricate numbers game.

SELECT BIBLIOGRAPHY

Atherton, M. (2003), *Opening Up*, Coronet Books.

Bannister, J., Lamb, A. (1996), *Allan Lamb: My Autobiography*, HarperCollinsWillow.

Botham, I., Hayter, P. (2001), *Botham's Century*, HarperCollinsWillow.

D'Oliveira, B. (1982), *Time to Declare: An Autobiography*, Star.

Donald, A., Murphy, P. (2000), *Allan Donald: White Lightning*, HarperCollinsWillow.

Greig, T., Lee, A. (1980), *Tony Greig: My Story*, Hutchinson.

Hick, G. (1991), *Graeme Hick: My Early Life*, Macmillan.

Moss, S. (2006), *Wisden Anthology 1978-2006: Cricket's Age of Revolution*, John Wisden & Co. Ltd.

Oborne, P. (2004), *Basil D'Oliveira: Cricket and Controversy*, Little, Brown.

Pietersen, K. (2006), *Kevin Pietersen: Crossing the Boundary*, Ebury Press.

Procter, M. (1981), *Mike Procter and Cricket*, Pelham Books.

Richards, B. (1978), *The Barry Richards Story*, Faber and Faber.

Smith, R., Crace, J. (1993), *Robin Smith: The Quest for Number One*, Boxtree Ltd.

Wilde, S. (1995), *Letting Rip: The Fast Bowling Threat from Lillee to Waqar*, Weidenfeld & Nicholson.